Santa Clara County Free Library

REFERENCE

D1572083

The Water King
Anthony Chabot

(Oakland Public Library, Oakland History Room)

"A Water King"

"By the above caption we do not refer to the storm king, clerk of the weather, or any other pluvial monarch, but to A. Chabot, the superintendent of the Contra Costa Water Company. It is no fulsom adulation that prompts us to assent that as a clear headed, sagacious, and capable manager of waterworks, he has not his equal on the Pacific Coast. Like all other men, he must be judged by the success that crowns his works."

Oakland Daily Transcript, July 15, 1876

The Water King

Anthony Chabot:

His Life and Times

by

Sherwood D. Burgess

Panorama West Publishing
Davis, California
1992

Library of Congress Catalog Card Number: 91–068105
ISBN 0–932857–04–3

Cover design by Lydia D. Schlosser

Panorama West Publishing
P.O. Box 2008
Davis, California 95617
Phone: (916) 756-7177
Fax: (916) 756-7188

Preface

His name is scattered over the San Francisco Bay Area. A few examples: Chabot College, Hayward; Chabot Observatory, Oakland; Lake Chabot, San Leandro; Anthony Chabot Regional Park; Lake Chabot, Vallejo. Almost all Bay Area residents recognize the name of Anthony Chabot. Most know that he had something to do with the water supply. Otherwise, little is known about the man whose contemporaries gave him the title "The Water King!"

In fact, the water systems of San Francisco, San Jose, Vallejo, and, especially, Oakland trace their roots to systems that Chabot helped to develop during the third quarter of the nineteenth century. Reservoirs of these primeval water companies still dot the hills around the bay. Some are still in use.

But Chabot was in the water business before he developed the water companies that lubricated the growth of the parched, infant communities around San Francisco Bay. In the early 1850s, near Nevada City, he was the first miner to use a hose to wash auriferous soil into gullies and flumes where the gold could settle out. He thus developed the principle of hydraulic mining. In Sierra County Chabot built miles of water ditches and flumes to bring water to the miners. He even built his own sawmills to supply lumber for his flumes.

Chabot was not only a water man. Despite his lack of formal education, this self-made, restless, French-Canadian immigrant had widespread interests. He invested heavily in industry and agriculture. Many prominent West Coast industries owe their origins to Chabot's shrewd investments. Tourists at Long Beach, Washington, still visit the "Anthony Chabot Cranberry Bog," the first on the West Coast.

Next to water, Chabot is best known for his philanthropy. He gave a considerable portion of his wealth to charity and to community projects in Oakland. Chabot Observatory, an existing monument to his generosity, is still visited by 30,000 people each year.

Very little has been written about this man who played such a prominent role in the Bay Area. Aside from a few articles, often inaccurate, and my master's thesis on the early history of the Oakland water supply, there is little readily available material.

This biography is historically sound. The sources for Chabot's major activities, projects, geographical locations, personality, family members, community relations, the names and backgrounds of his associates, and similar facts are cited in the Notes. But I have also taken the liberty to use circumstantial evidence and the historical background of the era to breathe life into The Water King. Thus, I sincerely hope that both the serious scholar and the general reader will enjoy this book.

Acknowledgments

I wish to convey my gratitude to the many people who have made this book possible.

Words cannot adequately express my appreciation for the help and support given to me by my family. My wife, Connie, spent endless hours proofreading, assisting me in libraries, and, most important, offering constructive criticisms of the manuscript. Without her help, encouragement, and evaluations the book might never have been finished. My daughter, Dennise, proofread the entire manuscript and, along with my daughter, Pamela, and Pamela's husband, George, supported and encouraged me throughout the entire project. My loving thanks to all of you.

My thanks also go out to five other persons who gave generously of their time to assist me.

Ms. Kay Clegg, of Santa Rosa, California, is a distant relative of Henry Pierce, who was a close business associate of Chabot. Ms. Clegg graciously sent me copies of her Pierce family archives that related to Chabot. Her manuscripts provided valuable information about Chabot's personality and his activities in the East.

Mrs. Ruth Chaplin, former librarian of the Steep Falls, Maine, library, most hospitably greeted my wife and me at the library and had pertinent materials arranged for us when we visited there. Both before and during our visit, she provided us with information concerning the nearby town of Standish where Chabot married, and lost, his first wife. Her help made possible much of the story on Chabot's first marriage.

Mr. Larry Weathers, former editor of *The Sou'wester,* the publication of the Pacific County Historical Society, South Bend, Washington, generously sent me copies of his own research materials on the Chabot Cranberry Bog, as well as printed articles on the subject. My section on the cranberry bog owes much to his kindness.

Dr. Kingsley Whiteman, Director of the Chabot Observatory, Oakland, made the observatory archives available to me. Mr. Carter Roberts, observatory archivist, took the time to mark and set aside for me the pertinent materials in the collection. The cooperation of these two gentlemen not only furnished me with information concerning the founding of the observatory, but also added insight into Chabot's personality.

I sincerely thank William Sturm for all of his help in the Oakland Public Library's Oakland History Room; Emily Miles, New Bern, N.C. library, for information on early tanneries in New Bern; and all the helpful personnel in the San Francisco Public Library's history room; the San Jose Public Library's California room; the Vallejo Public Library; the Library of the Society of California Pioneers; the California Historical Society Library; Sutro Library; Bancroft Library; the San Francisco Maritime Museum; the Portland (Maine) Public Library; the Maine Historical Society Library; Maine State Archives; York Institute, Saco, Maine; and numerous county court houses.

Sherwood D. Burgess
Concord, California
October, 1991

Contents

Preface   *v*

Acknowledgments   *vii*

1   Ambitous Youth   1

2   Forty-Niner   11

3   First Hydraulic Miner   20

4   Ditches and Sawmills   33

5   San Francisco   45

6   Eastern Interlude   60

7   Discovers Oakland   70

8   Temescal Dam   84

9   San Jose and Vallejo   97

10   Thirsty Oakland   112

11   Oakland Saved   124

12   Capitalist and Gentleman Farmer   139

13   Philanthropist   153

14   Oakland Mourns   166

Epilogue   170

Endnotes
Source materials for each chapter   177

Index   193

CHAPTER 1

Ambitious Youth

A n early winter storm swept across San Francisco Bay and pelted the muddy embankment that now blocked the flow of San Leandro Creek. Flumes from the hills upstream were pouring torrents of dirt and gravel over the clay core of the new dam. Dozens of horses driven by Chinese laborers ran back and forth over the embankment, compacting the sodden mass. Other workers were clearing trees and brush from the canyon walls above the small lake growing at the base of the dam. Tunnels were being bored through the cliffs at the end of the dam to connect the reservoir with the water mains that had already been laid to the drought-stricken city. The welfare of over 25,000 people depended upon this project. Water must reach Oakland before its meager supply ran out next summer.

The slight, graying, sixty-two-year old Frenchman sloshed through the mud in his hip boots. He pulled his coat tightly around him and tried to shield his small, wire-rimmed spectacles with his hat. His chief engineer, William Boardman, trailed after him, frantically urging the older man to go home.

Anthony Chabot ignored his assistant. This was his dam, his dream. It would be the greatest accomplishment of a long, productive career. He had personally supervised this job every day for the past year. You didn't build dams sitting in the president's office and letting your engineer do the job! Whether the summer of 1876 would be a disaster or the beginning of a new era for his adopted city depended on him. He would make a tidy $100,000 for himself on this project and possibly much more. He was not called the "Water King" because of engineers like Boardman, or paper pushers like his vice president, Henry Pierce. He had made his fortune through his natural talents and drive. He was a better engineer than Boardman, a better businessman than Pierce. And they both knew it.

His career began at age 14 during another storm when he had quietly slipped away from the Jesuit school at Chambly. Always restless, impatient with restrictions, disinterested in formal education, young Antoine had done poorly at the parish school of La Presentation about seven miles north of St. Hyacinthe, Quebec. He was born August 13, 1813, on a farm in Presentation Parish. His parents were solid French-Canadians. The Chabots had been prominent citizens since the earliest days of Quebec.[1] Although his father, Joseph, was comfortably well-off, he expected each of his thirteen children to do his share of work on the farm. But farm work, like school work, bored young Antoine. He wanted to enter business or commerce. But his father patiently explained that since the Act of 1791, which united French Quebec with English-speaking Upper Canada, the English merchants of Montreal completely dominated business, commerce, and government. A young French lad would have no chance at all in those fields. The French-speaking *Canadiens* of Quebec were mostly farmers. Some of the better educated entered law or the priesthood. But every year thousands of disgruntled *Canadiens* migrated to the United States, the bustling land of opportunity.

Finally, the elder Chabot sent his quiet, but very strong-willed, son to a Jesuit school at Chambly, on the Richelieu River about 25 miles southwest of St. Hyacinthe. There the boy would learn to be more cooperative; hopefully, he might then enter the clergy, or become a lawyer or a doctor—professions that were open to the French-Canadians.

This was a mistake. It lasted scarcely a year. Antoine was not a student. Throughout his life he was never one to reduce his thoughts to writing. The stubborn lad also would not accept the strict regulations and discipline of the black friars. The strong, dogmatic, religious emphasis permanently turned Antoine away from the church.

The glowering sky darkened his cell-like room. He had just received some spending money from his father. It was now or never! With determination Antoine rolled his meager belongings in a blanket. He thoughtfully fingered the coins in his pocket. They must last him a long time. Darkness and rain covered his unceremonious departure. The slight, dark-eyed French boy trudged confidently southward, ankle-deep in mud, along the rain-swollen Richelieu. The rain dripped from his high hat and long coattails. Many French and English armies had used this route to invade America. All had failed to reach New York City. Antoine Chabot would succeed![2]

A begrimed, tattered, discouraged youth trod the busy streets of Manhattan. Antoine had reached his destination after a four-hundred-mile trek from Quebec. His money was gone, and he was hungry and exhausted. He could only speak or understand a few words of English. He hungrily looked at the food-laden markets and the well-fed people entering luxurious restaurants. Antoine was too proud to beg and he would never steal. He probably could have made himself understood in the teeming foreign slum areas. But those crime-ridden neighborhoods frightened and disgusted him.

Fate was good to him. A farmer trading his produce in the market area spotted the homeless youth and took pity on him. He fed him and, after a conversation involving some English, some French, and much sign language, took the boy to his farm in central Manhattan. There Antoine agreed to work for the farmer for a year in return for his necessities and a small wage. Fate seemed to condemn him to farm life.[3]

But this year introduced Antoine to America. The young French lad had the opportunity to live with an American family near New York City, and to learn American customs and business methods. Most important, he learned the language, although his strong accent identified him as a Frenchman all of his life.

The booming city of New York in 1827, with 125,000 people, was larger than Chabot had ever imagined. The streets were lined with three-and-four story stone houses and hundreds of shops and businesses. The city was fringed on two sides with forests of tall masts of ships flying every flag of the world. The Hudson was smudged with black smoke billowing from side-wheeler steamers marching to and from Albany. The recently completed Erie Canal connected the Hudson with the Mississippi Valley, and New York had become a port of world importance. Each day more buildings and homes were spreading northward up the island; and some visionaries predicted that the city would some day reach Harlem, and would smother the farms in the central part of the island.[4]

The impressionable youth must have noticed the well-dressed ladies and gentlemen leaving their Broadway mansions and strolling toward the filigreed spire of Trinity Church which dominated the city. He also watched the wealthy alight from their splendid carriages outside the ornate Park Theater or at the resplendent Castle Garden concert hall. Although Antoine had little interest in religion or the arts, he was impressed with what money could buy. He liked to break up the little currency he had saved into small coins so he would seem to have more money to jingle in his pockets. Antoine Chabot would not always be a farm boy![5]

But there was another side of life in the dynamic America of the late 1820's. The New York slum areas were filled with hapless immigrants who were preyed upon by the dregs of society. Murderers and thieves abounded in alleys choked with filth and debris. Had Antoine not met his farmer benefactor, he might have drifted into these humanity-choked slums. While he never showed pity for the slouthful or criminal, he recognized that people, especially women, could be victims of circumstances beyond their control. In later years when Antoine made his fortune, he gave much of it to the worthy poor.

When his year on the farm had ended, Antoine could have settled in New York. There were innumerable opportunities for an ambitious young man in that busy city. But, always restless, the French youth decided to travel to the southern states, where the winters were mild, to make his fortune.

In contrast to the hungry, forlorn boy who had arrived in New York footsore and exhausted just a year before, a self-assured, confident young man now traveled southward. It was an exciting time to travel in America. Everyone seemed on the move. Swarms of boisterous people, entire families with all their belongings piled on wagons, turned westward off the north-south highway to take the new turnpikes and canals toward the hazy, blue mountains rising in the west. But the conservatively dressed Antoine had no inclination to don a coonskin hat and venture westward. He had no desire to clear the land and build a house with a rifle at the ready in case of Indians. He had had enough farming. At this time of his life, in fact during most of his life, money was his objective. A position in business or commerce attracted Antoine far more than a cabin in the wilderness.

As Antoine traveled deeper into the South, the busy mill towns, commercial cities, and small farms of New Jersey and Pennsylvania gave way to ever-larger plantations, worked by black slaves, in Maryland, and Virginia. Opportunities for an ambitious freeman were slim. The disillusioned youth headed for the North Carolina coast where he hoped to find a position in one of the coastal cities.

The small port city of New Bern lay on the south bank of the Neuse River. Sweating blacks were unloading cattle hides from a three-masted square rigger. Near the dock a large, low, brick building with water tanks atop its roof sprawled along the river bank and discharged dirty, brown water into the sparkling Neuse. A nauseous odor permeated the air around the building. Chabot learned that the hides came from California, a Mexican province on the Pacific Coast, and the building was a tannery owned by Daniel Shackleford who also had a saddle and harness shop near the town market. From his farm experience Antoine had a slight knowledge of leather goods. He decided to visit Mr. Shackleford.

The tall, graying, Daniel Shackleford critically eyed the serious young Frenchman, who no doubt assured him that he might be small, but that he had done heavy work. Antoine did not just want a "job," but a chance to work his way up in the business. He understood that this meant starting at the bottom where the work would be difficult and disagreeable. Shackleford would be a hard taskmaster. His products had a fine reputation, although his personal life left a bit to be desired. A father of several grown children, the former chief magistrate of the town had scandalized the community by leaving his wife and marrying a girl no older than his own daughters. But Antoine was not interested in his employer's private life. He saw only the opportunity to advance himself in a lucrative business.

The hours were long. The work was heavy and disagreeable. The superintendent, Brice Battle, an intellectual young man, fond of literature and mathematics, viewed the poorly educated, ambitious Frenchman with disdain and, possibly, jealousy. He probably assigned Antoine every dirty job in the plant. Young Chabot carried the heavy, smelly, salted hides from the dock to the wagons, and spent untold hours over the huge tanks that softened the stiff hides. He removed the salt, blood, flesh, and dirt and scraped off the hair. After soaking the hides for days in lime water and tanning solutions, he smoothed and stretched them. There was not a job that Battle did not give the Frenchman, but, in the process, Antoine thoroughly learned the business.

Then one day Brice Battle married. His long, intellectual nose could no longer stand the stench of the tannery. With little notice to his employer, he took his new bride off to Alabama. Antoine Chabot became superintendent.[6]

Antoine could have settled in New Bern and possibly bought into the tannery. But there were long-range drawbacks. The growing number of large cotton plantations were driving the local farmers with their cattle herds farther back into the mountains. Hides from California or the northern states were increasingly expensive, and the tanneries of New England were more labor efficient. New Bern's ambitious free laborers were moving westward and their places were being taken by ne'er-do-wells.

But, most important, Antoine, barely 20 years of age, decided that he did not want to spend his life in that dusty little town. His old wanderlust was again getting to him. He, too, was pulled by the lure of the West, but not by grubbing on its cheap lands. Endless profits could be made in the Mississippi Valley through supplying the farmers with the eastern manufactured goods that were pouring westward into the Valley over the turnpikes, canals, and rivers. Some quite conservative investors were even predicting that steam engines would soon be pulling wagons on rails connecting the East and West. Additional profits could be made by shipping the farmers' products to Eastern and world markets. The Mississippi Valley appeared to offer the aspiring Frenchman far greater opportunities than New Bern.

The main road across the Deep South from the Carolinas to the Mississippi passed great plantations with magnificent white manor houses. But behind the facades were rows of slave cabins whose occupants worked the well-tended cotton fields. Scattered among the great plantations were smaller farms with leather-faced yeomen and their careworn wives working lush, productive fields. But their farm houses were usually unpainted, fence rails sagged, and barns, often bulging with corn, leaned crazily. These independent farmers were frequently hard-drinking, crude, and violent. Cities, small and few in number, were dominated by the planters. Transportation was poor. Roads were generally unimproved, and navigable rivers and canals were almost non-existent. One 125-mile railroad from Charleston to Hamburg, which Antoine saw as he crossed South Carolina, was an exception. Antoine Chabot was not tempted to settle in the Southeast.[7]

But the young Frenchman was not disappointed in the Mississippi Valley where, with one brief interlude, he was to remain until 1849. He could give rein to his wanderlust and restlessness, traveling from place to place and engaging in numerous enterprises as his changing moods dictated. Although he put down no roots in the Valley, he emerged a wealthy man.

His first view of the Mississippi was likely from New Orleans where the highway across the south ended. This was the biggest city Antoine had seen since he left New York. He would naturally have gravitated to the already famed *Vieux Carre*, or French Quarter, with its two- and three-story buildings with balconies adorned with wrought iron railings. But Antoine's main interest lay in the American section along the river where the bustling wharves, warehouses, banks, and commercial establishments offered opportunities for an ambitious young man. River steamers unloaded Yankee produce from the expanding west and cotton and sugar cane from southern plantations. These goods were transshipped on ocean-going vessels to every part of the world. Goods were bought, sold, financed, and shipped at a frantic pace.

This melting pot of Southern, Latin, and Northern cultures was the commercial mart of the new West. Antoine soon recognized the opportunities of the Mississippi Valley.

Chabot observed the commerce of the main artery of the West as his paddlewheel steamer plowed northward through the muddy current of the Mississippi. The river was crowded with crafts of every description, from puffing stern-wheelers to keelboats, flatboats, and crude rafts, all elbowing their way along the tortuous, narrowing, tree-lined waterway. The wharves of budding southern river ports, such as Vicksburg and Memphis, were piled high with bales of cotton and stacks of lumber ready for shipment to New Orleans and thence to the seaports of the world. At Cairo, Illinois, swarms of boats of all types, carrying pioneers and produce from the Northeast, rode the flood of the Ohio as it poured into the Mississippi. Farther up-river St. Louis was growing into the gateway to the West as settlers swarmed into the fertile lands of Missouri, and the more adventurous fur trappers began eyeing the distant Rocky Mountains.

Much of the reason for this prosperity was due to the fiscal policy of President Jackson. The President withdrew government funds from the conservatively governed Bank of the United States and poured the funds into small state banks. Flimsy, wildcat banks spread throughout the west granting speculative loans on western lands and issuing their own notes which circulated as currency. State governments were borrowing heavily for internal improvements. Although he was too conservative to approve of Jackson's policy, Antoine was always ready to make a profit. He rode the wave of the fragile western prosperity, and through shrewd investments became a prosperous young man.[8]

About ten years after his departure from Quebec, Antoine for the first time felt successful enough to contact his family. He did so by sending a childhood sweetheart a clipping from a newspaper reporting that he owned a steamboat. Chabot was never one to write letters.[9]

In 1837 the prosperity ground to a sudden halt. Bank loans and state bank notes in circulation had far outstripped hard money. The government demanded cash payments for new land sales. English exporters began demanding cash for their products. Financial panic ensued. Banks collapsed. Land sales slowed. An oversupply of cotton and other produce piled on the docks with no buyers. Eastern factories closed. Western steamboats sat idle. Antoine quickly decided to pull out until the panic blew over. Again he thought of home and family. Taking his remaining liquid assets with him, the prodigal son returned.[10]

CHAPTER 2

Forty-Niner

Joseph Chabot looked up from his work in the fields. He was tired, graying, and bent from his life on the farm. His older boys had left home. He was helped with the lighter chores by his unmarried daughters and his ten-year-old son, Remi. And even the slight, thin-faced Remi was growing restless. Ever since he had seen the newpaper clipping about Antoine's steamboat, Remi was getting that faraway look in his sparkling dark eyes. He was no longer his father's zealous helper. Joseph sadly realized that his youngest son would not want to inherit the farm.

Remi watched the cloud of dust from the south as the stage approached from St. Hyacinthe on its way to Sorel, where the Richelieu joined the St. Lawrence. He waved to the driver as the coach pulled to a stop. Remi ran down the path to the gate to get the mail, papers, or whatever the driver had for the Chabots. But, instead, the door opened and a dapper young man in business attire stepped down. Joseph watched bewildered as the stranger put his hands on the shoulders of the boy, and Remi let out a shriek and threw his arms around the man. The coach pulled away as Remi excitedly led Antoine by the hand up the path.

The well-to-do Antoine, now 25, must have overwhelmed his family with tales of his travels and adventures as Remi listened in rapt admiration to this fabulous brother he had never seen. His mother scolded him for running away and not writing for ten years. Antoine protested that he had never liked to write. He visited old friends and neighbors. There had been many changes.

Even his former sweetheart to whom he had sent the clipping was likely now married. The excitement over Antoine's return soon died down.

Life on the farm resumed its normal activity. To his father's disappointment, Antoine did not put on his work clothes and join him in the fields. Instead, dressed in his business suit, he took the stage to St. Hyacinthe. He pretentiously explained to his puzzled parents that he was looking into a business venture.

On his trip home he had idly watched the herds of cattle roaming Quebec's green fields. Antoine had previously taken no interest in Quebec's cattle. They always reminded him of the irksome tasks of milking the cows and cleaning the barn. But now he thought of the smelly hides in the tannery at New Bern. While changing stages in St. Hyacinthe, he waited on the bridge and watched the Yamaska River flowing northward on its way to the St. Lawrence. Chabot was always fascinated by rivers and flowing water. As he leaned on the railing, he was reminded of the Neuse River that had supplied the tannery at New Bern.

A new venture raced through his active mind. Cattle for hides, plenty of flowing water to wash and process the hides, and a local labor supply in the community—all added up to a tannery! Chabot had the technical know-how and the business experience. He could invest a little capital and borrow the balance. He could make money right at home and be able to help his parents without working on the farm.

Antoine jumped feverishly into the project. He selected a site about 10 miles below St. Hyacinthe, where the river supplied ideal water power. He contacted landowners, suppliers of building materials, and financial institutions. The smiling, bright-eyed, little Remi trailed after him and was an apt pupil of business management. If Remi were only a few years older, Antoine would like him as a business partner.

But the months of planning and negotiations did not get the tannery built. The depression had spread to England and Canada. Credit was tight in the Canadian money markets, and Chabot was not going to put all his money in one venture. Throughout his lifetime Chabot's many projects were built mainly with borrowed funds.

But even worse was the winter! Antoine had spent considerable time in the balmy southern United States. And even the colder areas of the Mississippi Valley were warm compared to Quebec. Antoine could rough it when he had to, and during his life he often had to, but he enjoyed his creature comforts. Also, by this time he may have felt confined in the small community. It was not much better than New Bern! Restlessly, he paced the floor of the austere, cold, farmhouse, his mind racing with new plans which did not involve Quebec.

The long winter finally passed. Economic news from the United States was still grim. Money was very tight and unemployment was high. But in the Mississippi Valley there were signs of recovery as unemployed eastern workers moved westward toward the inexpensive, boundless lands of the West. Antoine decided to get in on the ground floor of a new prosperity. He gave up his plans for the tannery, and in 1839 bade his family goodbye. Remi wanted to go with him, but the boy was much too young. As Chabot stepped aboard the stage, he assured his crestfallen brother that someday they would be partners. Anthony would keep that promise![1]

Restlessly Chabot roamed the valley for another ten years. St. Louis was the center of the new western movement which leapfrogged the earlier settlements and began farming the endless plains that stretched toward the Rockies. Mountain Men explored the western mountains, mapped the passes that led to the Pacific, and boisterously returned down the Missouri River to St.Louis in boats loaded with furs. By the mid-forties wagon trains were

carrying settlers to Oregon and California, despite the fact that
Oregon was claimed by England, and California was a Mexican
possession. Settlers were also pouring into the Republic of Texas,
ignoring the protests of Mexico. Antoine was among those
shrewd investors who made their fortunes in the Mississippi
Valley by supplying the needs of these hearty disciples of
"Manifest Destiny" which carried the American flag to the shores
of the Pacific.

Antoine spent a brief time in the Republic of Texas. Everyone
knew that it would soon become a state of the Union. Chabot was
offered a position as superintendent of a large plantation. This
gave him experience in management which he would use in the
next decade. But despite Antoine's lifelong quest for money, he
always had compassion for the unfortunate. He could not have
been happy overseeing slaves. He was soon back in the Valley
where he drifted to New Orleans.[2]

In 1846 the United States annexed Texas. War with Mexico
ensued. By the Treaty of Guadalupe Hidalgo in 1848, the United
States annexed California. Antoine was in New Orleans in December, 1848, when the big news broke: Gold had been discovered in the newly conquered territory![3]

The news caused pandemonium in New Orleans' commercial
circles. Ripples of excitement even swept the usually placid
Chabot. His restlessness had not been satisfied by his short-lived
Texas venture. He now envisioned the opportunity to visit a
distant, almost fabulous, land where he could acquire far more
wealth than he could ever make in the Mississippi Valley.

Without really waiting for confirmation of the news, Antoine
and some of his associates began making plans to set out for the
gold fields as soon as possible. Chabot's first thought was to form
a mining partnership with Remi. Antoine immediately sent
money to a friend in St. Louis with instructions to arrange for

Remi to travel overland and join him in the California mines. But as word spread of the hardships and dangers of the overland trail, Antoine became concerned that Remi's youth and inability to speak English might expose his young brother to serious hardships. So, instead, he reluctantly decided to finance an older brother, Toussaint, who lived in Rochester, New York.[4]

Chabot feared that time was running out! Already the inhabitants of California had flocked to the hills and were scooping up the nuggets. Crowded shiploads of gold seekers would soon be sailing from every East-Coast port. Most of them would take the long four-to-eight month, hazardous journey around Cape Horn. Wagon trains were converging on St. Joseph and other overland jumping-off places in Missouri. But it would be autumn before they could reach the gold fields. Chabot and his companions recognized the advantage of their southern location. They looked forward to a short 1,700-mile voyage to Panama, a few-days' trek across the fifty-mile Isthmus to the Pacific Coast, and another thirty-day voyage from Panama to San Francisco. In two months or less they could be mining gold.

Antoine and his companions secured accomodations on the steamer, *Galveston.* Although the craft was not very large and did not appear too seaworthy, the agent assured them that it was perfectly sound for such a short voyage. On February 2, 1849, after repeated frustrating delays, Chabot finally stood at the stern of the ship and watched New Orleans disappear from view. Packed with 200 men, the first argonauts to sail from New Orleans, the frail little craft picked its way down the murky, brown Mississippi, past innumerable lush, green islands, to the Gulf of Mexico.[5]

The voyage across the Gulf and through the Yucatan Channel was smooth. Despite the crowded conditions, Antoine, who had likely purchased good accomodations, was enjoying the voyage.

But when they entered the Caribbean, he was driven below decks as a storm arose and battered the tiny ship unmercifully. The ship escaped destruction only by sailing into the Gulf of Honduras and taking refuge in the tiny, tropical port of Belize. Their vessel battered and leaking, the dispirited argonauts found miserable quarters ashore and impatiently awaited another ship which might take them to Panama. But no relief vessel arrived. After six galling weeks, during which they envisioned all the gold in California being snatched up before their arrival, the travelers in desperation helped the crew patch up the craft. Antoine had a hair-raising voyage along the Central American coast, as the *Galveston* limped toward Panama.[6]

In late March, the gold seekers disembarked from their leaky steamer in the palm-thatched, humid, jungle town of Chagres and prepared to cross the Isthmus. But Antoine encountered more obstacles. The only way to ascend the Chagres River was by pole-propelled dugout canoes whose slovenly owners charged outrageous prices on a take-it or leave-it basis. Fortunately, Chabot had the money to hire the best of the miserable crafts. It was said that only the wealthy should take the Panama route to California.[7]

After slow-moving, insolent porters finally sorted the travelers' baggage and put it in the right canoes, the group began the difficult and hazardous crossing. Chabot spent three, wretched, sweltering days swatting mosquitoes as the canoes slowly ascended the turgid, jungle-lined Chagres River. At night he stretched out on the muddy river bank or huddled against a tree. Despite the steaming heat, he covered himself from head to foot against the ferocious insects. At the head of navigation high in the mountains, the passengers were put ashore in a clearing. Their baggage was unceremoniously thrown on the muddy ground while the canoes glided back downstream and pack-mule drivers watched in sullen silence.

A new delay! More haggling and cajoling! This time Antoine's dark eyes blazed as he angrily negotiated for space on the hard, bumpy back of a mud-covered mule. The truculent animal bumped and slithered on muddy, precarious trails through rain-soaked jungles swarming with poisonous insects and reptiles. But Chabot's tired face suddenly beamed with excitement when the bedraggled party reached the summit of the cordillera. From there he saw the sparkling, blue Pacific just a few, easy, down-hill miles away.

But the wait in the ancient, walled city of Panama was a new ordeal. The city was packed with gold-seekers who had passed Chabot's party while they were stranded at Belize. The mass of humanity overflowed the city walls into a bamboo and canvas shantytown which was swept by malaria and dysentary. Antoine joined thousands of disheartened, sick, and quarrelsome argonauts who forlornly paced the beach awaiting the sight of a ship.[8]

Two modern mail steamers, the *California* and the *Oregon*, had been sent around the Horn before the news of the gold rush had reached New York. But these ships had departed Panama for San Francisco before Chabot arrived. Antoine cursed his many delays. He had also missed some sailing ships. There was only one small bark, the *Equator*, ready to sail north. It could hold only 137 passengers, and Antoine's name was far down on the waiting list.[9]

Chabot stood dejectedly on the beach and watched the tiny ship slowly disappear in the calm, azure Gulf of Panama carrying its fortunate passengers toward the California gold fields. It was almost April. Rumor had it that the mail steamers would soon return from San Francisco. But they were already overdue and overbooked. Antoine was not sure he could get aboard.

He wandered glumly along the wharves in the old part of the city. A little brig, the *Josephine*, was loading cargo marked

"San Francisco." The ship flew the flag of New Grenada (later, Colombia) of which Panama was a province. He went aboard. Would they take passengers? Captain Matilla shook his head. It would be a long, uncomfortable voyage. Chabot was stubborn and persistent, and he had ample funds. Captain Matilla relented. Others soon found the brig. With 80 passengers, the little *Josephine* set sail on April 20.[10]

The two-masted, square-rigged, tiny craft could not sail directly against the prevailing winds that blew steadily from the north. Only by making wide tacks far out to sea could it make progress up the coast. Week after irritating week Antoine paced the deck. He was not the philosophic type who could patiently watch the waves and the sea birds. But finally after a 90-day, exasperating, but uneventful, voyage, the Frenchman sighted the Golden Gate on Wednesday, July 18, 1849.[11]

Antoine observed the breathtaking vista of the enormous blue bay dotted with islands and surrounded by arid, oak-studded plains and redwood-capped hills. He did not realize the role he was destined to play in the urban development of this vast basin. As the ship sailed slowly around Black Point toward Yerba Buena Cove, Antoine was startled by his first sight of San Francisco. Hundreds of abandoned, deserted ships filled the tiny cove at the foot of a tall, barren hill covered with shanties and tents along a grid of dusty, dirt streets. Slowly, the ship edged its way toward a wharf.

As the gangplank was lowered, most of the crew pushed the passengers aside and rushed wildly off the ship, asking the dock hands for directions to the gold fields. Along with the other gold rush ships, the deserted *Josephine* bobbed in the crowded cove for months. It was finally purchased by Joseph Morehead who used the craft on an abortive filibustering expedition to Mexico in 1851. The *Josephine* was later sold and sailed up the Napa River where it was ignominiously anchored to the bank and used as a wharf and storeship until it rotted away.[12]

Antoine again had to haggle with insolent stevadores who demanded outrageous prices for taking his baggage to a hotel. He viewed with distaste a two-story, clapboard hotel which was located on the hill near the old Mexican plaza, now named Portsmouth Square. His room was possibly a tiny, second-floor cubicle with a small, hard bed and little else, and he was actually fortunate to have that. The less affluent new arrivals often had to sleep in vacant lots. On the hotel's first floor, gamblers and prostitutes cavorted noisily all night to the tune of a strident brass band. But San Francisco, even at this early date, had good restaurants serving the foods of many nationalities. Antoine soon found these places, and was fortunate to be able to afford the prices.

The city was tumultuous as new buildings were being thrown up everywhere. Squealing wagons loaded with redwood lumber from the hills across the bay noisily dumped their cargoes at the building sites, while the merchandise that would fill the unfinished buildings littered the streets. Although a decade later Chabot would be a prominent name in San Francisco, Antoine could now only think of getting away from this bedlam and heading for the gold fields.

CHAPTER 3

First Hydraulic Miner

In San Francisco rumors spread with lightning speed. In every bar, hotel lobby, assay house, or wherever men gathered, the latest news from the mines poured in. The current excitement was generated by a strike on Deer Creek, a tributary of the Yuba, in the northern mining area. There was plenty of gold, but, as yet, not too many miners had made their way up there. They were still clustered at Parks Bar, on the Yuba above Nye's Landing. Antoine, sitting alone at a table amid the hubbub, cocked an ear.

Chabot had remained in San Francisco many weeks, investigating the tempting opportunities that abounded in business and trade, as well as in mining. But he had finally decided that greater possibilities existed in the mining country. Now he was impatient to get to the mines. But he did not wish to go to an overworked area, nor did he wish to be led on a wild-goose chase by a rumor. But the Deer Creek strike seemed to present the ideal opportunity.

Galvanized into action, the erect, slim Frenchman strode into the U.S. Mail Packet Line's office on the waterfront at the foot of Sacramento Street. Here he paid $50 for deck passage on a small schooner which carried supplies to Sacramento, the jumping-off point to the mines. Early next morning Chabot embarked on the small craft carrying, in addition to his bedroll and a few personal belongings, a week's rations—mainly bread, crackers, cheese, bologna, and wine.[1]

The cool, high fog dissipated as the boat sailed northward on the whitecapped bay and turned eastward into Carquinez Straits.

The brisk, summer wind from the fog-shrouded ocean carried the little schooner swiftly between the brown, rolling hills that lined the Straits. The pilot edged the craft toward a small embarcadero below the town of Benicia which sprawled at the foot of the sun-burned hills to the north of the windy waterway. Also docking at the wharf was Dr. Semple's ferry from the embryonic town of Martinez that nestled in a valley on the south bank of the Straits. Miners traveling from the south used the old Spanish trail from Mission San Jose to Martinez and then took Semple's ferry to Benicia. From that budding community they could reach Sacramento, or the mines, by land or by river schooner.

The tinder-dry, twin peaks of Mount Diablo dominated the landscape to the south and looked down upon the broiling Central Valley. Innumerable waterways flowed into the Straits from the hot, flat, delta to the east. The pilot instinctively guided his craft past dozens of sloughs and tule-clad islands up the main channel of the Sacramento River.

The heat became unbearable as the sea breeze died and the boat sluggishly fought the growing current. At times it made no headway at all. Each night the little ship was tied to any convenient tree at the edge of the River, while man-eating mosquitoes, as bad as any at Panama, chewed upon the adventurers. Chabot bemoaned the fact that river steamers were then being built in San Francisco, but none were yet in service.

Finally, the schooner pulled toward the east bank of the River and tied up to a sycamore tree. The riverbank, piled with lumber and bales of goods, served as a wharf. The newborn Sacramento City consisted mainly of a few clapboard buildings and tents that lined Front Street along the Sacramento River. A few other scattered hotels, stores, and residences graced largely imaginary streets that pointed eastward across the sun-drenched plain toward Sutter's Fort.

At Front and J Streets Antoine entered the establishment of Sam Brannan and Company. Brannan regularly advertised in the San Francisco papers that he sold mining supplies at San Francisco prices. Sam was a Mormon elder who had led a party of 200 Mormons to California by sea in 1846. He was the character, who, in May of 1848, had precipitated the gold rush by racing into Yerba Buena waving a quinine bottle full of gold while shouting, "Gold! Gold! Gold from the American River!" He no doubt assured Antoine that the hottest gold strike was on Deer Creek about 60 miles northeast of Sacramento by a very rough road. A better route was by boat up the Feather River to Nye's landing on the Yuba and then by a much shorter, easier road to Deer Creek.[2]

As Antoine sailed northward through the clear waters of the Feather River, his dark eyes sparkled in anticipation of a new adventure. He wondered what opportunities lay ahead for him in those formidable mountains to the east. He was confident that he would make a fortune and would soon sail back down this river a wealthier man.

The formerly peaceful Nye's ranch was a bedlam of feverish activity when Chabot landed on the north shore of the Yuba at its confluence with the Feather. Rollicking prospective miners were refreshing themselves before their treks to the mines, and eager developers and surveyors were busily transforming this pastoral setting into a city, which would soon be called Marysville. Here Chabot would have joined a wagon train headed for Parks Bar about 12 parched miles up the Yuba. It was there in May, 1848, that the Contra Costa rancher, John Marsh, had discovered gold on the stream and opened a store. In September genial David Parks had opened his own store in competition with the dour, cantankerous Marsh. Marsh became ill and returned to his ranch with $40,000 in gold. Parks left later with $85,000.[3]

About seven months after he left New Orleans, Chabot approached Parks Bar. The usually placid Frenchman could scarcely contain his excitement. He had finally spotted a group of gold miners! Antoine looked down on the crystal-clear, rocky stream that meandered through the low, rolling brown hills. A few scrubby trees and bushes lined its banks. The afternoon sun flashed on the swirling pans of hundreds of bearded miners, their bronzed faces shielded by wide-brimmed hats, squatting on the shores of the creek. They were intently looking at the mixture of water, gravel, and, hopefully, flecks of gold in their pans. Loud cheers echoed along the river when an exuberant miner held up a large nugget before he dropped it into a can or canvas bag. Curses could be heard as disappointed miners flung worthless gravel back into the river and started the panning process all over again. Other miners shoveled dry dirt from the banks of the creek and carried it in sacks to what looked like a cradle sitting with its bottom in the river. They dumped dirt into the contraption, which they rocked, and hoped that gold would settle out amid the cleats on its bottom while the lighter dirt was washed away. Chabot likely wondered, as he watched, if it would not be better to divert water from the creek to the diggings, rather than carry the dirt to the cradle in the creek.

Near sundown, hot and bedraggled, but with his shoulders squared, Chabot walked confidently into a shabby hotel. After refreshing himself, he must have been tempted to unpack his shiny new pan and start mining. But upon sober consideration, Antoine decided that he did not care to push his way into this worked-over area.

The next day he crossed the river and followed a wagon road eastward into tree-covered hills. On Squirrel Creek, about 15 miles from Parks Bar, a few crude buildings and tents were scattered along the road. A scrawled sign proclaimed the camp of Rough and Ready. Captain A.A. Townsend, from Wisconsin, had named the community after his Mexican War commander, and current President of the United States, "Old Rough and Ready," General Zachary Taylor. Clusters of miners in the ravine below the road stared silently at the newcomers who felt it prudent to keep moving.[4]

A few miles beyond Rough and Ready, Antoine looked down on a wooded valley through which Deer Creek flowed westerly, and Gold Run Creek wandered northward into Deer Creek. There were scattered miners along Gold Run and others on Deer Creek—enough activity to indicate that gold was available, but, as yet, there was plenty of elbow room.

On the north side of Deer Creek, above its confluence with Gold Run, a few tents, brush shanties, and log cabins were scattered on pine-covered ridges between the ravines that ran from a range of hills to the creek. To the east, "Dr." A.B. Caldwell, who already had a store about four miles downstream, was building the first store in the infant community—Dr. Caldwell's "Upper Store." His log-and-canvas establishment,

In his early days in Nevada City, Chabot not only used long toms, but also manufactured and leased them out. (Bancroft Library.)

near present Nevada and High Streets, appeared to specialize in whisky, pork, moldy biscuits, gingerbread, and assorted mining supplies.

Chabot, who had avoided wilderness areas in the East, moved into this primitive community with some trepidation. At first there were no civilizing influences such as law enforcement officers, schools, churches, or families. The miners worked all day in a fever of excitement in the ravines and creekbed, or in the flats on present lower Main Street known as Deer Creek Dry Diggings. At night they would unwind in their tents and cabins amid the pines on the hills above the creek. Antoine could see the lanterns in the dimly lit dwellings, while sounds of laughter, shouting, fiddling, and singing would float down the slopes. Occasionally the merriment turned to angry snarls when a gambler cheated, or a miner resented a practical joke, and a fight, often fatal, broke out. Chabot stayed well away from such activities.[5]

Antoine created no great stir among the turbulent elements. He quietly staked a claim in Buckeye Ravine, between present-day Main and Coyote Streets, about a quarter mile above Deer Creek, beyond the area then being worked by the other miners. Chabot would work the Buckeye Ravine area during most of his stay in Nevada City. Although the French newcomer had yet to pan his first flake of gold, within three years he would revolutionize the placer mining industry.[6]

During the fall of 1849, in addition to swarms of miners, married couples and business people arrived in increasing numbers. In October C.H. Stamp of Tennessee arrived with his wife, children, and sister, and built a cabin a few hundred yards down Buckeye Ravine from Chabot's claim. Mr. and Mrs. Penn arrived soon afterwards. Buildings began to spring up on Broad Street. The nucleus of an orderly community began to develop.

To Chabot it had looked so simple—squatting beside a creek, swirling light gravel and water out of the pan and picking out the heavier flakes of gold. But it was not that easy! With a slouch hat covering his dark-brown hair, trousers tucked into his heavy boots, Antoine squatted on the muddy bank day after day, his feet wet and cold, his legs and back aching. But still it was rather fascinating at first. His dark eyes were glued on the gravel in the revolving pan awaiting that fleck of color. Then Chabot felt the excitement common to all miners as he eagerly picked out the flakes, and, sometimes, sizable nuggets. Like most of the miners, he often panned from several ounces to a pound of gold per day. But he soon grew restless. As he swirled his pan, Chabot's active mind was planning easier and more profitable ways to extract gold.

Then came the rains. The winter of 1849-50 was one of the wettest on record. Heavy rains started in late October and seldom let up. Deer Creek, a trickling stream in the fall, turned into a raging torrent. A sizable rivulet rushed down Buckeye Ravine. Unusually heavy snows swept the foothills and remained on the ground until March. Prices soared as Dr. Caldwell's supply wagons mired down in the muddy roads. Hundreds of the Deer Creek miners fled over the slippery roads toward Sacramento only to find that fledgling town under several feet of water. Although Antoine disliked the rain and snow, he joined the many determined argonauts who remained that winter. Chabot worked his claim in Buckeye Ravine at every break in the weather.[7]

During the winter Chabot was startled to see his brother, Toussaint, sloshing up the ravine. It was a happy reunion for the two brothers who had not seen each other for many years. Antoine had financed his older brother's overland trip and looked forward to a long association. For a few weeks the brothers panned gold together as they talked of future plans. But the partnership did not last long. Antoine was soft spoken and quiet, but he stubbornly wanted his own way. Possibly Toussaint had the same traits. Whatever the reason, Toussaint took off on his own for a new gold strike to the north in Trinity County. He eventually settled in Walla Walla, Washington Territory.[8]

In 1850 Antoine was overjoyed when the smiling face of his favorite sibling, Remi, appeared at the entrance of his rustic quarters. Remi was 22 years old, but knew little English, and despite Antoine's earlier admonition that he was too young, had joined a wagon train for California. The lighthearted, cheerful Remi and the serious, willful Antoine seemed to complement each other. The two brothers were to work together for most of the rest of their lives.[9]

Spring weather finally appeared and miners began to pour into the area known as Caldwell's Upper Store, or Deer Creek Dry Diggings. By March, 1850, over 1,000 miners had swarmed into the area. A town government became necessary for a safe and orderly development of the community. Mr. Stamp was elected *Alcalde* under Mexican law. (California had not been admitted as a state; so Mexican law was still accepted.) The miners, recalling the white winter, decided to call the town Nevada.

During 1850 the community grew rapidly, and its streets were soon lined with hotels, saloons, gambling dens, brothels, stores, homes, and even a Methodist Church. The following year the town was incorporated as a city, and it was quickly rebuilt after a disastrous fire. At that time Antoine was delighted by the establishment of a French restaurant and hotel by Charles Gaudin. At last, he thought, as he enjoyed his first good meal in the mountains, civilization was coming to Nevada City.[10]

Meanwhile, the restless mind of our Frenchman was planning new mining ventures. Buckeye Ravine would nearly dry up by late summer, making panning difficult. And Chabot wanted no more of that life style. Plenty of gold was left. The veins of rock filled with gold-bearing quartz lay deep inside the earth. But these veins could only be reached by expensive mining methods. A quartz mine was dug near Deer Creek just east of Nevada City; and Grass Valley, a few miles south of Deer Creek, became the site of several deep gold mines. At this time Antoine was not interested in quartz mining, although later in life he invested in several mines.

Antoine's interest centered in the so-called "dry diggings," or gravels, such as were found in the hills and ravines around Nevada City. These gravels contained placer, or water borne, gold deposits washed down from lodes or veins by ancient rivers. Over the ages as the Sierras rose, these stream beds had been covered by layers of silt and gravel, and were often as much as 100 feet beneath the surface. Other, less rich, but substantial, auriferous deposits had been laid down by flooding streams in later times and were closer to the surface.

To reach the rich, deep deposits, some miners tried to dig shafts into the earth to find the ancient gravels. These "coyote holes," which looked from a distance like animal burrows, were tedious, dangerous, and expensive. As the miner descended, he shoveled the dirt into square wooden buckets attached to a windlass operated by his partner. The dirt was emptied near the opening and later hauled to the creek where it was washed, and any gold was extracted. Many of these holes went down to bedrock where extensive horizontal shafts were dug. Although some coyote miners struck it rich, this method held no interest for Chabot. Antoine was not going to be a mole.

Carrying the dirt from lower grade surface deposits to a cradle in the creek was also no answer. Chabot watched his neighbors, Mr. and Mrs. Penn, the wife working beside her husband, digging the dirt on the bank and carrying it like animals

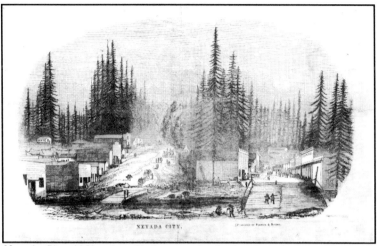

Nevada City, 1852, when Chabot was developing the principle of hydraulic mining by using a hose without a nozzle in nearby Buckeye Ravine. (Bancroft Library.)

in sacks on their backs to the cradle in the creek. They made a good living. In the spring of 1850 Mrs. Penn could afford to open a boarding house, the first building in town built with sawn lumber. But Antoine was not going to be a pack horse.[11]

He had concluded that the water had to be brought to the dry diggings, not vice-versa. Antoine decided to invest some of his gold to construct a flume to tap water from a stream at a higher elevation and carry it to his claim in Buckeye Ravine. This was the beginning of Chabot's life-long obsession with hydraulics. He then built several long toms. Through these long, three-sided boxes, with perforated plates or sieves bent upward at the ends of the toms, he ran water from his flume. His crews then shoveled dirt and gravel from nearby banks into the toms. The heavy gold was caught by the sieves, while the lighter dirt and water would flow off into the ravine.[12]

Antoine's concept was not unique, and as water flumes and ditches proliferated throughout the Nevada City area, Chabot recognized a demand for long toms. So, in addition to the toms he built for himself, he constructed several others which he leased to miners for eight dollars a day. Chabot soon gained a reputation in Nevada City, not only as a successful miner, but, also, as an able businessman. An associate wrote: "Although he was a spare, slim man, his grip was phenomenal. When he shook hands to close an agreement, his associate felt that his hand was in a vice. And it was also well known that Chabot's mental grip was equally tenacious."[13]

Although the long tom was more efficient than coyote diggings or the cradle, it still required shoveling dirt and carrying it to the tom. Chabot soon recognized the superiority of ground sluicing, which was growing in popularity since its introduction in 1850.

This method actually goes back to the days of Roman mining in Spain. Water from a flume or ditch was tapped at a higher elevation and flowed down a declivity, or over a bank, while miners shoveled the nearby dirt into the water, or would often loosen a bank with picks to hasten its erosion. The gravels were then carried by the flowing water to a nearby ravine in which sluice boxes had been placed to catch the gold. These devices were shallow three-sided boxes about 12 feet long, two feet deep, and about 18 inches wide. They had cleats across the bottom to catch the heavy gold, and the miners often used mercury to amalgamate and settle out the smaller gold particles. Several boxes were often fitted together in order to extract the maximum amount of gold. The run-off, or tailings, would wash down the ravine. Sometimes impounded water would be released all at once and would sweep with great force across an expanse of gravel. This method was called "booming."[14]

Although Chabot had eagerly adopted ground sluicing, he was not entirely convinced that it was the most efficient method of using water power. He still had to hire large numbers of men to pick and shovel the dirt, and it used an excessive amount of expensive water to move a relatively small amount of soil. If only more efficient use could be made of water power to move the dirt with a minimum of shoveling and picking! Antoine Chabot then conceived one of the most innovative developments in the history of mining.

In April, 1852, on Buckeye Hill, Chabot connected a long wooden box, strengthened with clamps, to a flume at a higher elevation. This box could withstand a pressure of 60 feet. To this high-pressure water source he connected a canvas hose about 40-feet long and four or five inches in diameter. He directed the hose on loose dirt and gravel, or on gravel that had been picked off high banks by hand, and washed it into the sluice boxes using a minimum of water and manpower. He also found it useful for cleaning off bedrock. His hose could wash gravels that sluiced water could not reach, and thus reduced the need to shovel and

The environmental disaster that ultimately resulted when others added a nozzle to Chabot's experiments with a hose. (Bancroft Library.)

carry dirt. The greater pressure of the hose could wash heavier gravels and undercut banks. Although his hose could not wash away hillsides, Antoine successfully used his primitive hydraulic mining process until early 1853. No other miner copied his system that season.

But in the spring of 1853 one of Chabot's partners, Edward E. Matteson, a native of Rhode Island who was living in Connecticut when he heard of the gold rush, carried Chabot's hydraulic concept one step further. On his claim on American Hill, Matteson attached a crude nozzle to a hose. With stronger pressure and greater range, his hose could blast away entire hillsides. Matteson's nozzle was quickly imitated and greatly improved upon, and hydraulic mining soon developed into one of the most effective, and controversial, mining techniques in history.[15]

When Matteson claimed to have originated hydraulic mining, Chabot said nothing. Antoine never looked for honors. He would let future historians argue whether the first use of the hose, or the addition of a nozzle to the hose, actually opened the era of hydraulic mining. He only knew that his hose had washed a great amount of gold into his purse. It had made him a wealthy man.

He jingled the gold coins in his pockets and thought of his days in New York when he had jingled pennies. He had come a long way! But it was time to move on.

CHAPTER 4

Ditches & Sawmills

In the summer of 1853 Anthony Chabot stepped from the Marysville Stage in front of the Rabbit Creek Hotel in the Sierra County mining camp of Rabbit Creek Diggings (La Porte since 1857). The hotel, the only frame building in Rabbit Creek, was built in the previous year by Eli Lester on the dusty road that twisted on northward up the eight-mile grade to the camp of Gibsonville.[1]

Chabot attracted little attention as he quietly edged his way past unwashed, raucous miners and brightly painted ladies in the tumultuous bar. Anthony was not a man who stood out in a crowd. He had neither the stature nor the gregarious personality to lend him a commanding presence. But he would quickly become known, as he had in Nevada City, through his accomplishments. And, as in Nevada City, the modest little Frenchman would soon grow restless and silently slip away, much richer, leaving few records about himself for posterity.

By now he had anglicized his first name, dropping the "Antoine." Although his accent would always betray his ancestry, "Anthony" would be advantageous in dealing with miners, many of whom had strong, even violent, prejudices against Frenchmen. In later life he often reverted to the "Antoine;" but he usually signed his name, "A. Chabot." [2]

Chabot did not come to Sierra County to mine gold. The Slate Creek Valley, into which Rabbit Creek flowed, had had a number of mining camps since 1850; but the easily panned gold was running out and miners were leaving. At almost double the elevation of Nevada City, the severe winters also discouraged the individual gold seekers. In this rugged area expensive group-mining ventures were necessary. They had to bring water from higher elevations to the dry diggings for long toms, ground sluicing, and, by 1855, hydraulic mining. In fact, two short ditches had been dug before Chabot arrived. So Anthony brought capital and hydraulic know-how, not a miner's pan, to Rabbit Creek.

With his characteristic drive and energy, Chabot jumped into two complementary activities, water diversion and sawmills. Anthony recognized that artificial waterways to the diggings near Rabbit Creek could be constructed from the upper tributaries of the South Fork of the Feather River, and from the higher eleva-tions of Slate Creek near Gibsonville and Whiskey. This water could be conveyed several miles down the Slate Valley to Rabbit Creek, St. Louis, and to such picturesque sounding places as Secret Diggings, Bernard Diggings, Spanish Flat, Sears Dig-gings, and Howland Flat. These waterways would need miles of wooden flumes as well as ditches, and Anthony quickly realized the profitablity of having his own sawmills.[3]

In the summer of 1853 a group of 32 miners had pooled their resources and formed the "Feather River and Spanish Flat Ditch-ing Company." They planned to construct a ditch to bring water from the Feather River to their dry diggings on Spanish Flat below the town of Rabbit Creek. But the work progressed slowly, and the miners became discouraged as funds ran low. The dis-heartened, bearded argonauts, their hands blistered from digging and hammering, needed both money and advice.

In October the leader of the company, J.H. Kilburn, sought help from Chabot, who was well known for his previous hydrau-lic activities in Nevada City. While Anthony could give advice, he was hesitant to loan all of the $5,000 cash needed by Kilburn at

La Porte, Sierra County, was known as "Rabbit Creek Diggings" when Chabot was there from 1853-1855. It took its present name in 1857. (Bancroft Library.)

that time. He was sinking much of his capital into two expensive steam sawmills down in Slate Valley. But he had the good fortune to meet B.O. Williams, an old acquaintance from Nevada City. Williams, who had also built ditches near Nevada City, had also come to Sierra County with some capital, which he would be willing to invest for a good return. It was agreed that Williams would lend the miners $3,000 and that Chabot would lend them $2,000. Interest rates were running from three to five percent per month, payable monthly, with any overdue interest becoming part of principal. Not a bad rate of return!

Promissory notes payable to Williams and Chabot were se-cured by a mortgage from the Feather River and Spanish Flat

Ditching Company, conveying to Williams and Chabot the partially constructed ditch and any appurtenances, rents, and profits therefrom until the notes were paid. When Kilburn presented the terms to the tired, hungry miners, they lustily shouted their approval. The next day thirty-two men, with Kilburn at their head, lined up in front of the tiny office of Ben W. Shepard, Justice of the Peace. They tramped with muddy boots and sweat-soaked work clothes through the office. Each signed the document. Probably very few of the signatories understood the instrument, but all, except one, could write their names. The cash purchased the necessary supplies, equipment, and food. Work on the ditch resumed. By the following spring, water was flowing through the ditch to Spanish Flat, and the miners were happily sluicing. Chabot and Williams were paid off by the end of August.[4]

Meanwhile, the hyperactive Frenchman was looking for sawmill sites and ordering steam engines, saws, and other equipment. He finally selected two sites. One mill was located on Slate Creek near St. Louis, named by a homesick Missourian, and the other mill was on Rabbit Creek, about three miles away. Anthony had observed in Nevada County that sawmill operators flourished as mining camps grew into sizable towns and miles of wooden flumes were constructed. Down there, other entrepreneurs had established themselves in the lumber business while Chabot was enriching himself washing gold. But in Sierra County, where growing towns and expanding flumes were devouring lumber, Anthony was on the ground floor.

Two sawmills were an expensive proposition, and Chabot needed a partner with cash and sawmill expertise. He went into partnership with Adoniram J. Rigby, who had the two prerequisites. Each man owned a one-half interest in each mill.[5]

Chabot's sawmills, known as the St. Louis Steam Saw Mill

and the Rabbit Creek Steam Saw Mill, were large-scale operations. They not only included the mills, but also extensive yards
for logs and cut lumber, housing for dozens of employees,
stables, cattle, mules, and wagons. When the streams were high,
logs could be floated down to the mills; but the cut lumber had
to be hauled by ox carts over the steep, muddy roads to its
destination.

During the winter of 1853-54 Chabot lived at the mill near St.
Louis. For a man who had left Canada and sought out the southern
United States because he disliked Quebec's winters, Chabot had
picked a rough area in which to make a living. The Slate Valley,
about 5,000 feet elevation, can be cold. Snow was soon covering
Bald Mountain and other nearby peaks and drifted into the valley.
The mill worked except in the worst weather. Chabot huddled in
a clapboard shack which he shared with his brother, Remi, and
cursed the weather. When he supervised the operation of the mill,
usually from the warmth of the steam boilers, he clad himself in
woolen pants, which he stuffed into his heavy boots, a flannel
shirt, wool jacket, and a slouch hat pulled over his ears. Young
Remi, who had lived longer and more recently on the Quebec
farm, took the cold weather in his stride. But Anthony determined
that this was the last winter he would spend in the mountains.

The mills were very profitable and filled Chabot's pockets.
Orders were heavy as the area boomed, and lumber sold at
premium prices. Labor was plentiful at $3.00 a day, which was by
then the standard wage in the mining country.[6] But after a year,
the little Frenchman became restless. The mills were too confin-
ing, and he did not want another winter in the Sierra. Moving
water was his great love, not sawing up trees.

Rigby jumped at his partner's proposition. Chabot would sell
his half interest in both mills for $13,000. As this might strap
Rigby for operating cash, Chabot generously took only $2,500 in

cash, and the balance of the $10,500 in 13 promissory notes with interest at the low rate of 2.25 percent per month. One note was to be paid on the first of each month between December 1, 1854 and December 1, 1855. These notes were secured by a mortgage giving Chabot a three-fourth interest in both mills until the notes were paid. Rigby eagerly signed the agreements on September 1, 1854.[7]

But the sawmill operator soon rued the day that he made the contract. He was unable to keep up his payments and his interest costs soared. He still owed Chabot a considerable sum in early 1856. In May Anthony released his interest in the St. Louis mill back to Rigby, but kept his mortgage on the Rabbit Creek mill. Finally, on July 15, 1856, Rigby managed to send his final payment to his ex-partner who was now in San Francisco. Chabot was very profitably out of the sawmill business.[8]

While he was in the sawmill business, Chabot was also developing water ditches. In the early 1850's, with almost no legal formalities, one could divert unclaimed water from a stream, and construct the ditches and flumes which carried the water across public property. Nor was there a limit on the amount of water a person could use. Regardless of the length of the ditch, he only needed to drive stakes along the route of the project, post notices of his intentions, and actually commence work on the waterway. The operator of the ditch could use the water personally, or he could sell it to others at whatever price the market would bear. Only if the waterway were sold or mortgaged did its existence become a matter of public record.[9]

Chabot had either a proprietory or a creditor's interest in at least eight water projects in the Slate Creek area and in at least one ditch in Yuba County. His ditches crisscrossed the entire Slate Creek mining area. Some were short canals, two or three miles in length, running from Rabbit Creek to Secret Diggings or

from Slate Creek to Gibsonville. But longer waterways extended
from upper Slate Creek, or from the south fork of the Feather
River, to the diggings below Rabbit Creek. These lengthier
projects were more complicated and included both ditches and
elevated flumes. Anthony's involvement in bringing water to the
dry diggings in the Slate Valley covered the period from his
arrival in mid-1853 until after he settled in San Francisco in mid-
1856.

Anthony was not only a self-made hydraulic engineer, but he
also had a natural instinct for making shrewd, profitable investments. This money-making talent had supported him for several
years in the Mississippi Valley. In some cases, as with Kilburn,
Chabot would loan a few thousand to a ditch operator, take a
mortgage on the entire project as security, and charge the usual
three to five percent monthly interest. Annualized, this interest
amounted to 36 to 60 percent. He also made two such loans in
July of 1856 after he had settled in San Francisco. But he usually
entered these water ventures on a proprietorship basis.[10]

As these projects required considerable capital, Anthony usually went into a water project with partners. Eli Lester, the hotel
proprietor, John Thompson, who may have sailed from New
Orleans with Chabot on the *Galveston*,[11] and Archibald Smith
joined Chabot in water projects. After building the ditch and
operating it profitably for a year or two, Anthony would get
restless, lose interest, and offer to sell his share to his partner. In
the case of John Thompson, Chabot was paid $5,000 cash for his
share. But the other situations were similar to the sawmill deal
with Rigby. Chabot accepted payment in promissory notes,
drawing the customary monthly interest, and secured with a
mortgage on his partner's share of the business. Most of these
notes were paid off on time, but when they were delinquent
Anthony was further enriched by the compounded interest. There

is no evidence that Anthony ever foreclosed on a mortgage.

By 1855, as hydraulic mining became more prevalent and the demand for water greatly increased, recorded water claims began to supplant the informal process of staking out a ditch. In March, 1855, Chabot and J.F. McManus filed a water claim with Sierra County for all the previously undiverted water of the South Fork of the Feather River above Grass Valley, along with the right to conduct it to the Rabbit Creek mining area. They also claimed lands for dams and reservoirs and a 400-foot wide right-of-way for a ditch.[12]

During a three-year period, Chabot issued a total of at least $35,000 worth of promissory notes secured by recorded mortgages on water ditches or sawmills in Sierra County. The average note ran about a year at three percent monthly interest. From these notes alone he must have netted at least $12,000. If we add to this his interest from unrecorded loans, and substantial profits from his sales of water and lumber, it is apparent that Chabot emerged from Sierra County much wealthier than when he left Nevada City.

In autumn 1854 the first storms blew from the west sprinkling the river valleys. As clouds reached the higher elevations, the rain turned to sleet and snow. Anthony's boots sunk into the muddy slush as he and Remi walked toward the warmth of Eli Lester's Rabbit Creek Hotel. Eli and Anthony had recently been partners in a water ditch. Eli had bought out the Frenchman and now owed him $2,400.

Anthony cursed in French while he brushed the cold sleet from his full beard with his wet, woolen glove as they tracked mud across the lobby and sat on a hard, wooden bench before a roaring fire. The lighthearted, younger brother could not keep a teasing smile from his thin face as he watched his serious older brother's discomfort. No more mountain winters for Anthony!

Eli brought them a hot drink. Remi readily agreed to remain in the mountains and take care of Anthony's affairs. It would also give the young Frenchman an opportunity to mine on his own and to start making his fortune.[13]

As his stage neared Parks Bar, Chabot must have been disturbed to see that the formerly clear, sparkling Yuba was brown and turgid. It was filled with gravel and silt that poured into the river from the hydraulic mines near Nevada City on Deer Creek and from the water cannon at Bloomfield on the South Yuba. He realized that next year the tailings from the Slate Creek mines would further pollute the river. Anthony remembered his excitement that April day in 1852, when he first washed loose gravel into a sluice box with a hose. It was so much quicker and easier than shoveling the dirt! And there had been no great destruction. It was Matteson who had first used the nozzle. But if there had been no hose....He was still musing as he arrived at Parks Bar and the muddy stream carried its alluvium on towards Marysville.

Over the next three decades Chabot's hydraulic process washed untold millions of dollars in gold into the economies of California and the United States. This contributed heavily toward saving the Union in the Civil War. But the process also washed millions of tons of silt into the rivers of central California which impeded navigation and caused destructive flooding of farmlands and cities. The ecological damage to vast areas of the Sierra is still evident today.[14]

Chabot spent a short time at Parks Bar. He sold his interest in a nearby ditch known as Prairie, or Chabot's, Ditch which ran about ten miles from Dry Creek to Prairie Diggings. He also had Remi arrange the sale of a ditch near Rabbit Creek to Anthony's former partner, John Thompson; and he sold out his interest in another Sierra County waterway he had jointly owned with his associate, Archibald Smith.[15]

In the summer of 1855, Anthony settled in Marysville. He had first passed through Marysville, when it was still Nye's Ranch, on his way to Nevada City in the fall of 1849. But the ranch's strategic location, on the east bank of the Feather and the north shore of the Yuba, attracted developers who bought the land and laid out a town in December, 1849. The town grew rapidly from 300 people in January, 1850, to 8,000 when Chabot settled there in 1855. Regular steamboat sailings to Sacramento and San Francisco, a telegraph line to San Francisco, and regular stage departures to the mines on Deer Creek and Slate Creek made this an ideal hub for the Frenchman's activities. From here he could phase out most of his investments in Sierra County and make contacts in San Francisco at the same time.[16]

It seemed good to be back in civilization. Anthony had demonstrated that he could rough it when necessary. He was happiest when he was supervising construction work, and had proudly listed his occupation in the Marysville City Directory as "Surveyor." But Chabot always enjoyed the amenities of city life. St. Kinsey's boarding house in Marysville seemed like a palace compared to the crude mountain hotels and the shacks that Chabot had endured over the past five years.[17]

The wily Frenchman felt that a town which had grown as rapidly as Marysville would certainly have a great future. So while he was divesting his interests in Sierra County and making inquiries concerning opportunities in San Francisco, he dabbled in Marysville real estate. He joined with Charles A. Keyser, a native of Maryland, who had arrived in California in 1852 and had settled in Marysville. Charles was employed as clerk of the U.S. Land Office, was a notary public, and, later, became an attorney.[18]

In August 1855 the partners purchased from Yuba County at public auction for $4,250 a corner lot on the south side of 3rd

Street and the west side of D Street. On this land they erected two brick buildings, a saloon and the Land Office Building where Keyser worked. The fact that Chabot and Keyser received rents from Keyser's employer, the United States government, seemed to raise no eyebrows in the free-wheeling capitalism of the 1850's.

The Marysville interlude did not last long. Chabot's optimism in the real estate market was not justified. Marysville's rate of growth greatly declined. When he sold his share of their property to Keyser in 1859, he made only $575 over his share of the purchase price, not including the rental income he received during that time.[19]

On July 11, 1856, Chabot purchased at the bargain price of $85 an 80-by 160-foot piece of undeveloped property on the outskirts. It was his last Marysville purchase. The next morning at 6:00 a.m. Anthony boarded the California Steam Navigation Company's river boat for San Francisco.[20]

From the deck he watched the smoke billow from the twin stacks, side by side, forward of the walking beam. His little freight boat on the Ohio, nearly 20 years ago, had not been as elegant as this one, but it had made money. As he sailed down the murky, brown Feather River, he turned his eyes eastward toward the dry, brown range of mountains silhouetted against the rising sun. Those mountains had been good to him and had rewarded him for the hard life he had led there. But he wanted no more of them. He hoped Remi was making good, and that he was also carefully looking after his older brother's remaining investments.

To avoid the chill morning air, Anthony stepped inside the cabin. On a wall was the schedule of the California Steam Navigation Company. Among the signatures at the bottom of the notice was that of John Bensley, director. Chabot knew that Bensley was planning a water company in San Francisco.

Anthony's eyes turned away from the Sierra Nevada and strained toward a hazy blue landform low on the south-western horizon. Beyond Mount Diablo lay San Francisco, a thirsty city.

CHAPTER 5

San Francisco

C habot found San Francisco completely changed from the
clapboard and canvas town where he had landed in '49.
After a few years of tumult, arson, murders, duels, cor-
ruption, and vigilantes, the city now had a substantial business
district with bustling brick office and warehouse buildings. Under the streets and buildings that now covered the cove where
Anthony first came ashore, many of the abandoned gold-rush
vessels lay buried forever. Residences, many of them palatial,

*Example of the San Francisco water supply, early 1850s, before Chabot,
Bensley, and Von Schmidt created the San Francisco City Water Works.*
(Bancroft Library.)

covered Rincon Hill and were stretching out over the hills and valleys to the north and west.

As he walked along the waterfront, Anthony watched with interest as a barge of the "Saucelito [sic] Water and Steam Tug Company" pumped water into two large redwood tanks on the abandoned ship, *Cordova*. The water came from springs on the ranch of Willam A. Richardson near Sausalito. At the foot of Sacramento Street another abandoned ship, the *Mentor*, advertised the sale of water. These and other water ships sold fresh water to vessels in the harbor as well as to individual customers.

Anthony also observed a large barrel mounted on a horsedrawn two-wheeled cart. Across the street stood a mule burdened with two smaller barrels. Busy young men wearing broad-brimmed sombreros filled buckets from spigots on the barrels, and hurriedly carried water into business establishments and homes. The young businessmen charged one dollar per bucket for their service, and would not sell their routes for under

San Francisco, 1851. There was no public water supply for the thirsty and combustible city. (Bancroft Library.)

$1,500. This water mostly came from local artesian wells. But many householders and businesses preferred to depend upon their own wells. However, in recent months the water level on the arid, sandy peninsula had dropped. The wells were dug deeper, but tragic accidents due to cave-ins occurred with increasing frequency.

Yes, as Anthony had heard in Marysville, San Francisco would soon become a thirsty city. Its growth would be stifled if it continued to rely on these primitive water sources. Not only would lack of water for domestic use become an insurmountable problem, but the hilly, inflammable city, without a high-pressure piped water system, would remain at the mercy of a fire. An ordinance required every householder to keep six buckets of water ready for fire, and a few cisterns were scattered about the city. But these measures had not prevented six major conflagrations in an 18-month period. Another fire could wipe out the city's future as a major metropolis.[1]

Chabot checked into "The Railroad House" (although at that time no railroad ran into San Francisco). This luxurious, four-story hotel that extended between Commercial and Clay streets, had a clock tower on the roof that was a city landmark. Anthony seems to have preferred hotel living; he had no home of his own until very late in his life.[2]

One of Anthony's first acts in San Francisco was to become an American citizen. This country had given him opportunities that he would never have had in English-dominated Quebec. Despite the anti-French sentiment among some of the miners in Nevada County, he had become a rich man through his own hard work and ingenuity. In cosmopolitan San Francisco, his French accent would be absolutely no barrier to his success. On October 7, 1856, Anthony Chabot quietly, yet proudly, displayed his naturalization papers to his acquaintances.[3]

Meanwhile, Chabot threw himself into the search for a water project. He learned that in March, 1851, Azro D. Merrifield had presented plans to the Common Council to pipe water from Mountain Lake into San Francisco. Mountain Lake, now a city park, was about a mile in circumference, and 150 feet above sea level, on the northwest side of the peninsula. In early 1852, Henry S. Dexter, who would later work with Chabot, was hired to survey routes from Mountain Lake to San Francisco. Dexter proposed running a 30-inch cast-iron main from the lake to the Golden Gate, and thence along the shoreline to a reservoir at North Beach.

The city approved the Mountain Lake Water Company's franchise in July, 1852, and gave the Company the unrealistic deadline of January, 1853, to complete the project. Work did not even get underway until early 1853, so the city extended the deadline to 1854. A complicated plan to tap the Lake below its surface caused delays and expense. It also appears that the Company officials deviated from Dexter's planned pipeline, and began work on a $300,000 brick-and-concrete water tunnel under the route of Pacific Avenue as far as Larkin. (The tunnel was still in existence in 1893.) Although another extension was granted by the city in 1854, the firm was in deep financial trouble when Chabot came to town in 1856. He would not risk his hard-earned money and his reputation in a poorly managed, failing business.[4]

In 1856 before Chabot arrived in San Francisco, George H. Ensign purchased some springs in a shallow depression known as Spring Valley on the north slope of Nob Hill on Mason Street just north of Washington. From these springs Ensign filled some cisterns and supplied water to carriers. He called his venture, "The Spring Valley Water Company." This enterprise appeared to be just one of many artesian-well companies with no future. Its 20,000-gallon daily supply would not start to provide San

Francisco's water needs. Chabot dismissed it from consideration.

But in May, 1857, after Anthony had committed himself to another company, Ensign ran a 1,500-foot hose connecting his mini-water works on Mason Street to a cistern at Stockton and Broadway. The cistern was for fire purposes, and Ensign benevolently provided the water to the city free of charge. Chabot likely shrugged off Ensign's act as a publicity stunt. He could not foresee that this was the beginning of an eight-year love affair between the grateful city and the Spring Valley Water Company. This upstart was to swamp Chabot's first municipal water venture.[5]

Since his arrival in San Francisco, and possibly before, Anthony had been attracted by the scheme of John Bensley to take over the franchise of the nearly defunct Mountain Lake Water Company, and to run pipes from that lake into San Francisco.

Born in upstate New York, a year before Chabot's birth in

John Bensley, Chabot's Associate, San Francisco City Water Works Company—often called "The Bensley Company." (Bancroft Library.)

Canada, Bensley was a typical mid-19th century entrepreneur. Like Chabot, he spent his youth before the gold rush in a variety of money-making enterprises. After serving as a captain during the Mexican War, Bensley was in New York when he heard of the California gold strike.

Bensley immediately booked passage around the Horn on one of the first steamers. Before he sailed, he chartered a bark, loaded it with goods and supplies, and ordered it to follow him to San Francisco. Bensley arrived in California in June, 1849, and went directly to Sacramento and built a store. His goods arrived aboard the bark, and John was soon making money selling supplies to the miners. He may well have met Chabot at this time. Bensley returned briefly to New York and bought two steam boats, which he sent to California for the river trade. In February, 1854, he helped organize the California Steam Navigation Company which consolidated all the steamer companies on the river.[6]

The slightly built, quiet Frenchman was drawn to the six-foot, broad shouldered, affable New Yorker. Anthony sensed that his own hydraulic experience, and considerable business acumen, combined with Bensley's management background, drive, and standing in the community, would make a strong combination. Together they surveyed the Mountain Lake area. The Mountain Lake Water Company still claimed the water rights to the lake even though the city had finally revoked its franchise.

Chabot and Bensley tried to circumvent the claims of the Mountain Lake Company by tapping nearby Lobos Creek. Although the waterway was in close proximity to the lake, Chabot and Bensley conjectured that Mountain Lake was not the source of Lobos Creek. The creek appeared to have its sources under the rolling sand dunes to the south, where Golden Gate Park now lies.[7]

To confirm their theory, the duo consulted Alexander W. Von

Schmidt, a Latvian-born engineer who had arrived in San Francisco in 1849, and, like Chabot, had constructed hydraulic projects in the mining country. The squint-eyed engineer ran his hand over his close-cropped hair, and thrust out his massive jaw, as he studied the windblown, barren, sandy landscape of the northwestern tip of the peninsula. He later dogmatically agreed that Lobos Creek did not drain Mountain Lake, and optimistically estimated the daily flow of the creek to be 22,500,000 gallons— enough to supply a city of 125,000 population with 20 gallons per person each day. Its bed overgrown with vegetation, and its flow reduced to a trickle, Lobos Creek still runs along the southwestern end of the Presidio and enters the ocean near the southern end of Baker Beach.[8]

As they observed the creek pouring into the sparkling waters of the Golden Gate, Anthony's dark eyes flashed with excitement. He had the system planned! Actually it was a modification of Dexter's plan for the Mountain Lake Company. A small diversion dam above the mouth of the creek could funnel its water into an inexpensive wooden flume, eliminating the need for an expensive pipeline. The flume, with a gradual slope, would carry the water along the shore of the Golden Gate and the Bay to a reservoir on a beach near San Francisco. Chabot had built dozens of similar flumes in the mountains. The obstacle of Fort Point could be overcome by tunneling through the promontory. Von Schmidt confirmed that the idea was feasible, and he was invited to join the project.

Enthusiastically the trio sprung into action. In early spring of 1857, Chabot, acting as superintendent, set a crew to work on a stone-and-earth dam across Lobos Creek. By the end of May the dam was substantially completed, and Chabot had already ordered the redwood lumber for the flume and had made some excavations along its route.[9] Von Schmidt attended to the survey

and technical engineering details. Bensley worked on such necessary legal matters as the certificate of incorporation, a franchise
from the city, and permission to run the flume on U.S. Army
property. The incorporation of the company took first priority, as
the three men were each fully liable as partners for the debts they
had incurred. At this time, the company was known as the
"Bensley Company," the name by which it was informally known
for the rest of its existence.

On June 15, 1857, the three men set their signatures to the
Certificate of Incorporation of the San Francisco City Water
Works and became its first trustees. The purpose of the corporation was to deliver pure, fresh water into the city and county of
San Francisco. The capital stock of $1,500,000 was divided into
3,000 shares at $500 a share. The articles were signed by John
Bensley, A.W. Von Schmidt, and A. Chabot, who were subse-
quently elected as president, secretary and chief engineer, and
superintendent, respectively.[10]

The San Francisco City Water Works was granted its first franchise on August 6, 1857 by Order #46 of the Board of Supervisors.
The company was to build a dam near the mouth of Lobos Creek, and
run an aqueduct along the shore of the bay to conduct water from the
dam to a two-million gallon reservoir on North Beach near the foot of
Taylor Street. The project was to be completed within one year, or the
works would be forfeited to the city. Within two years, two brick-and-
concrete distribution reservoirs were to be built at elevations of 100
and 200 feet above sea level with respective capacities of four million
and two million gallons. The firm was allowed a generous profit of
24% a year for five years on the actual cash capital invested. Thereafter, the profit would drop to 20%. The city was to be given free
water for fire and public purposes, except street sprinkling, and a
$2,000 public fountain was to be erected and supplied with water at
company expense.

The city fathers obviously had dreams of a publicly-owned water supply system, which were not to materialize until the following century. The franchise included provisions for an eventual city buy-out of the company.[11]

While the terms were not entirely favorable to the company, the trio felt that they could influence better legislation in the future. But now it was necessary to concentrate on the construction work which involved a seven-mile flume, a tunnel, and a two-million gallon receiving reservoir—all to be completed within a year. Superintendent Chabot needed help—not the help of a professional engineer, like Von Schmidt, but from a practical, working superintendent like himself. Anthony sent an urgent appeal to his best friend and partner, brother Remi.

The timing was perfect. Anthony no longer had investments in Sierra County for Remi to oversee. Remi had been involved in ditches and mining, and was doing quite well. But the big hydraulic mining companies were taking over the La Porte region, limiting the opportunities for the individual miner. Remi was ready to taste the amenities of civilization. In the winter of 1857-58, he was hired as assistant superintendent of the San Francisco City Water Works. Like his older brother, Remi became a naturalized citizen. He took his oath in April 1858.[12]

The brothers worked day and night on the aqueduct. The redwood flume was over four feet high and three feet wide, and had a slope of 30 inches per mile which permitted a steady flow of one mile per hour. The structure was covered with boards to prevent debris from the cliffs from falling into the water, and also to enable workmen to service the flume. (In later years it became a path for adventurous hikers.) It followed a tortuous route along the rugged shore. High wooden stilts carried the structure over indentations in the shoreline, while excavations were necessary where the flume crossed promontories. A tunnel had to be dug to carry the water through the promontory of Fort Point, as the Army was building a large fort at the water's edge which blocked the path of the flume. The old fortress may still be seen beneath the Golden Gate Bridge.[13]

By May, 1858, it was obvious that the work would not be completed by the unrealistic franchise deadline of August 6th. Chabot and his associates were faced with the possibility of forfeiting to the city, without compensation, their partially completed system, as well as all of their machinery, stockpile of pipes, and construction materials—the fruits of a year's labor and investment. While the Chabot brothers worked their crews at a feverish pace, Bensley bearded the supervisors.

The supervisors would not agree to eliminate the forfeiture provision in the franchise, nor change the size or location of the Taylor Street reservoir. But, on May 28, they did agree to reimburse the company for the cost of the works if they took it over. Thus, before the city could take the water company's property, an appropriations measure would have to be passed and probably tested in the courts—a lengthy procedure. The San Francisco City Water Works had a reprieve![14]

Anthony and his cohorts decided that the best strategy would be to ignore the construction details in the franchise and to get water into downtown San Francisco as soon as possible. A supply of pure, fresh water should win the favor of the citizens and cool off the supervisors.

On June 18, 1858, the Chabot brothers' flume rounded Black Point, near the foot of Van Ness. Here, in present day Aquatic Park, they began building a small receiving reservoir and pumping station. This was a half mile from the foot of Taylor Street where the franchise dictated a two-million gallon reservoir. Chabot's crews had already begun excavating a six-million gallon distributing reservoir at 110 feet elevation at Francisco and

San Francisco City Water Works' Pump House (small building with smoke stacks), Black Point, near foot of Van Ness. Water from flume, at right, was pumped into two reservoirs on Hyde Street Hill in background. (San Francisco Maritime National Historical Park.)

Hyde streets. At the same time plans were being drawn for a two-million gallon reservoir at 250 feet elevation at Greenwich and Hyde to serve the higher sections of the city.

Within a month the receiving reservoir began filling the partially completed Francisco Street Reservoir, and by early September Anthony was watching the dirt fly as water mains were being laid. On September 27, 1858, San Franciscans rejoiced as the first water flowed through the mains into their city. Largely due to the engineering efforts of the grave little Frenchman and his smiling, personable brother, San Francisco's watercarts would soon be *passé*.[15]

By the summer of 1859, the system was nearly completed. 40,000 feet of pipe had been laid in the city and 45 hydrants had been installed. The citzens no longer needed to keep fire buckets filled and at the ready. But the company had built its system exactly as it pleased, and not according to its franchise.

Faced with a *fait accompli,* the supervisors amended the franchise for the third time in August 1859. Anthony, John, and Alex smiled triumphantly as the board realistically voted to accept the system as it had already evolved. But smiles turned to frowns as the frustrated supervisors let the axe fall! The Bensley Company's profit schedule was drastically slashed, and the firm was required to pay five percent of its gross receipts to the city. A number of other irritating details were also included in the revised franchise. Clearly, the *detente* between the San Francisco City Water Works and the City and County of San Francisco was at an end.[16]

The San Francisco City Water Works reached its zenith in 1860. Its 74,000 feet of pipe and 100 hydrants monopolized the most thickly settled portions of the city and were being extended toward the outskirts. The pumping station, with two steam engines, had been completed near Black Point, west of present Ghirardelli Square. The solidly constructed brick building, with its prominent square smokestack, was operational for nearly a century. The landmark was torn down after World War II with the development of Aquatic Park. The reservoirs at Francisco and Hyde and at Greenwich and Hyde, though covered, are still in use. Although in the early 1860's it was replaced with an underground conduit from Fort Point to Black Point, Chabot's flume from Lobos Creek was used until 1893 as an additional water supply for the city and as the main source of water for the Presidio. The Chabot brothers left their mark on San Francisco![17]

Despite the benefits San Franciscans reaped from its new water supply, the Bensley Company's relations with the community rapidly deteriorated. There was a rash of customer complaints over the high prices charged for water that did not always taste pure and fresh. The firm also required its customers to pay the entire cost of connecting the service pipes from the street mains to the property lines. The company's right to enter its customers' premises at any time, to insure compliance with the San Francisco City Water Works' 18 pages of rules and regulations, was an added irritant.[18]

There was also internal dissension over management policy. In April, 1860, the strong-willed Von Schmidt left the company to join "a more vigorously administered concern." New faces appeared at the board meetings, including Henry S. Dexter, who had made the first surveys for the Mountain Lake Company. The following year Bensley himself was replaced as president by F.F. Low, although Bensley and Chabot still remained as trustees.[19]

To make matters worse, a fair-haired child was growing up in San Francisco's water world. Ensign's little works in Spring Valley had always fascinated San Franciscans. While Chabot was busily at work constructing the San Francisco Water Works' system, George Ensign was continuing to sell his water to water carriers and to fill, free of charge, the city's fire cistern at Stockton and Broadway. In the spring of 1858, the supervisors quietly granted Ensign a franchise to furnish San Francisco with water. But at that time the Spring Valley Company had too little water to be a viable competitor to Chabot and his associates.

A group of capitalists bought out George Ensign in 1860. The new group included William H. Tillinghast, president, and the Bensley company's turncoat, A.W. Von Schmidt, trustee and chief engineer. The new management announced grand plans which excited San Franciscans who were thoroughly unhappy with the old company. Tillinghast and Von Schmidt were going to exploit the vast San Mateo Creek watershed in San Mateo County. The Spring Valley Company immediately began work on dams, pipelines, and reservoirs which would provide almost unlimited water for San Francisco. During 1861 and '62 San Franciscans eagerly read the news of the pipeline creeping northward toward their city.

As the grand plan would take time, the Spring Valley Company quickly bought a little firm with water rights on Islias Creek. In 1861, 400,000 gallons per day were conveyed by a flume from the creek to a small reservoir at 16th and Brannan streets. Soon, nine miles of mains were laid in the city and a two-million gallon reservoir was completed at Market Street and Buchanan. Bensley and Chabot now had serious competition.[20]

Anthony Chabot was elected president of the beleaguered San Francisco City Water Works in late 1861. A third Chabot, brother John, joined the firm and was placed in charge of pipe manufacturing. Anthony attempted to improve the company's public image by lowering the water rates and ending the excessive service connection fees. But this was too little, too late. The Bensley Company had lost public confidence.

Then disaster struck! In January, 1862, during the worst winter storm on record, Chabot's receiving reservoir went dry. The pumps stopped. A mud slide along the coast had washed away part of the flume. Anthony eagerly shed his president's suit and donned rain gear and boots. He was soon racing, no doubt with Remi beside him, toward the Presidio with a repair crew. The little Frenchman braved the storm-swept coast, day and night, while he personally supervised the repairs.

Meanwhile, the reservoirs drained dry and the company's mains were empty. There was no water for the city's hydrants, and a fatal hotel fire resulted. Mayor Teschemacher and Fire Chief Scannel suggested that the two water companies pool their resources. Von Schmidt wrote Chabot a flowery, overly-friendly letter offering to connect the Spring Valley's main, free of charge, to the Bensley system. When President Chabot returned to his office two days later, he replied that the repairs had been made and the pumps would soon be started. He did not think there would be a need for the connection; but because of fears of accident, he would agree to it. He politely, but formally, thanked his former colleague for his friendly gesture. The accident cost the San Francisco Water Works $20,000.[21]

Soon after the connection was made, the Spring Valley customers complained that their water was muddy. Von Schmidt replied that it was due to mixing his water with that of the San Francisco City Water Works, which had a mud slide on its flume. The Bensley firm's popularity rating hit an all-time low. A few days later the *Mirror* wrote concerning the muddy water: "This disagreeable fact is thus accounted for. The Spring Valley Company, as full of benevolence as their reservoir is of limpid water, generously connected their pipes." The crisis over, the Spring Valley Company disconnected its pipes from those of its competitor.

For the next three years the press was full of praise for the Spring Valley Company, as its system brought San Mateo water into San Francisco. Hardly a kind word could be found for the Bensley Company, especially in 1864 after three Bensley employees were arrested for connecting their mains to Spring Valley's pipes and stealing its water. But the honeymoon between the city and Spring Valley soon ended. The quality of Spring Valley's water and its high rates disappointed the populace.

In January, 1865, the two companies merged and kept the Spring Valley name.[22] Both John Bensley and A.W. Von Schmidt lost their jobs in the process. But Chabot was long gone. He had resigned by mid-1862, sold his stock, and left San Francisco in disgust. It had not been a very happy, nor profitable, venture for Anthony. Remi remained in San Francisco as a broker. John remained for another year manufacturing pipes, a trade he taught Remi, and then disappeared.[23]

CHAPTER 6

Eastern Interlude

In early 1862 Chabot, upon bailing out of the floundering San Francisco City Water Company, embarked upon a three-year odyssey in the North-Eastern states.[1] The details of his business activities are quite vague, and the episode marks the nadir of his career. Anthony did, however, find the great love of his life in a remote town in Maine, but, tragically, he soon lost her.

It was during these years that Chabot's life became entwined with Henry Pierce, an early stockholder in the San Francisco City Water Company where the two men became acquainted. Pierce, about 14 years younger than Chabot, was born in Standish, Maine, a village 20 miles west of Portland. He was the second son in a family of five boys and a girl. In 1850 Henry arrived in San Francisco and opened a bakery where he was soon joined by a brother, William. Henry was aggressive and ambitious, and could be ruthless. He dabbled in many enterprises, including the water company, while the steady hand of William ran the bakery.

By 1861 both Anthony and Henry were restless. They discussed possible business opportunities in the East where the Civil War was then raging. They wondered if San Francisco had passed its peak. Pierce had connections in the East. His brother, Marshall, lived in Biddeford, Maine, just south of Portland; a married sister, Ann, resided in Lynn, Massachusetts; and he had distant relatives in Wisconsin. He also may have been homesick for the green, wooded, gentle hills of his Maine birthplace. Chabot and Pierce agreed to go East together and investigate projects that could utilize Anthony's engineering skills and Henry's business acumen.

Henry was eager to get started, but Chabot was desperately trying to hold the faltering water company together. They agreed that Henry would set out first, and Anthony would join him later. Henry left San Francisco in early 1861 and joined his brother in Biddeford. In the spring of 1862 he left Maine, apparently to meet Chabot in the Midwest.[2]

In early 1862, Chabot resigned as president of the water company and sold his stock. He then set out by stage across the country. The Central Pacific and Union Pacific railroads were then being planned. In less than a decade, iron rails would roughly follow the route of Chabot's stage. Upon reaching the railhead at St. Joseph, on the Missouri River, Chabot alighted from the stage and boarded a train to Chicago.

Chicago was already becoming the nation's rail hub. There Anthony changed trains and traveled 80 miles north to Milwaukee, Wisconsin, a growing port city on Lake Michigan. It was here that he likely joined Henry Pierce.

The booming town of about 50,000 people, 60 percent of whom were German, stretched along a crescent-shaped bay of the Lake at the confluence of the Milwaukee and Menomonee rivers. Branch railroad lines spread across the state and hauled the annual wheat harvest to the wharves of Milwaukee, making it one of the busiest grain ports in the world. The streets were crowded with drays and carriages, and the air was anything but sweet-smelling. The odor of manure vied with the stench from the slaughter houses on the Milwaukee River and the smell from the breweries.

But Anthony was not interested in air pollution. He was interested in the fact that, like most growing communities of that decade, the town would soon need a potable water supply. The once-pure Milwaukee River was now lined with slaughterhouses, barnyards and privies. And the town sewer system drained directly into the River. Even the hardiest Milwaukeeans had given up drinking river water. Numerous springs had once provided pure water, but they had dried up. Now the townfolk largely depended on shallow wells in their yards but, as in similar cities all across America at that time, the wells were competing with privies and stables for space.

As early as 1857 the Common Council had ordered that a municipal water company be established and had consulted a Chicago engineer, E.S. Chesbrough. But by 1862 nothing had been accomplished. Chabot drew up plans for a system, no doubt involving the use of Lake Michigan water. But the Westerners could arouse no interest in the plan. The people were happy with their wells. Although Anthony and Henry left town disappointed, their failure was a blessing. Ten years later when lake water was finally piped into the city, traces of Milwaukee River sewage were in the tap water. For years afterward the city struggled with this pollution problem.[3]

The two men next traveled to New York, passing near the booming, turbulent Pennsylvania oil fields. It was only three years since Edwin Drake had struck oil at Titusville, but already over 200 highly competitive oil companies were drilling along Oil Creek. Although Chabot had not considered investing in that disordered industry, he noted that all companies had one problem in common— getting their product to market.

Storage and transportation were acute. Coopers could not make barrels quickly enough to store the gushing oil. Thousands of teamsters moved the barrels over quagmire roads, a slow and expensive process. Barges loaded with oil barrels were floated down Oil Creek on freshets created by opening dams along the waterway. But this was a precarious method of moving oil. Boats often crashed into one another, spilling their cargo. In December, 1862, an ice pack smashed 350 boats, destroying 30,000 barrels of oil. The following spring a disasterous fire destroyed nearly 100 boats and burned down a bridge. Although railroads soon extended rails into the fields, teamsters or barges were still necessary to transport the oil to the railhead. And until the development of the horizontal, steel tank car in the late 1860's, much oil was lost from leaky and exploding wooden barrels on the railroad flatcars.

Chabot heard of a short pipeline, about 1,000-feet long that was being constructed from wells to a nearby refinery. Another pipeline, about five-miles long from wells to a railhead, was being proposed by Samuel Van Syckle. He was trying to raise $100,000 for the project, which was finally completed, despite sabotage by teamsters, in 1865.[4]

Anthony had even more grandiose ideas! He developed a plan for an oil pipeline from Pennsylvania to New York City. Water could be moved great distances by pumps and gravity. He had spent the past ten years moving water. So, why not crude oil? His plan no longer exists, but it was no doubt sound. Chabot was a first-rate hydraulic engineer. Both he and Henry were astute businessmen. But the project would cost more than the Californians could afford. If Van Syckle needed $100,000 for a five-mile line, a 300-mile pipeline would run into many millions. They presented the plan to New York capitalists and proposed a corporation to build and operate an oil pipeline. But the New Yorkers scoffed. The plan was too visionary! Impractical! The upstarts from the West knew nothing of the oil business! But most of the scoffers lived to see Chabot's plan for long distance pipelines become a reality.

Practically laughed out of New York, the discouraged Westerners headed for Maine, where Henry knew that Portland was having a water crisis.[5]

Chabot stood near the old 80-foot tall observatory on Portland's Munjoy Hill. To the north and east, dozens of green islands floated on the sparkling blue waters of Casco Bay. On the western horizon, beyond Back Cove, the White Mountains traced a thin, faint, irregular smudge. To the south and west, busy Portland lay on a tongue of land between Munjoy and Bramhall hills. The wharves, ships, and dingy warehouses that stretched along the Fore River bustled with activity. Tree-lined Congress Street, with its substantial brick homes and countless church spires, ran down Munjoy Hill, along the spine of the peninsula, and past the brownstone mansions on Bramhall Hill. It then wound eastward toward the back country.

Chabot mused that the peninsula was a small scale version of San Francisco, with a larger rainfall. But its water supply problem was much the same. As early as 1811, water was carried from wells and small streams from Munjoy Hill through log aqueducts and lead pipes into the town. However, most people depended on their own wells and cisterns which were kept full by a plentiful rainfall. But now the city was growing. Wells were becoming contaminated. The fire danger was acute. An adequate, piped, public water supply was becoming necessary.[6]

Anthony pictured distributing reservoirs on the hills at each end of the peninsula. But these reservoirs, Chabot knew from sad experience, would require a large source of supply—not local creeks or wells. A source was needed similar to the artificial lakes that the Spring Valley Company was tapping in San Mateo county, and which were swamping his Lobos Creek system.

Henry already had the answer to the supply problem. Sebago Lake, the second largest in Maine, lay about 23 miles northwest of Portland, and was only three miles from Henry's birth-place of Standish.

The two men set off in a buggy across the green, wooded, rolling countryside. Between the dense groves of multi-colored trees, red farm houses and barns dotted the landscape. An occasional village, such as Westbrook, Gorham, and Windham stretched quietly along the narrow, rutted, dirt road. Each town was marked by the white belfrey of its church rising over a cluster of white, green-shuttered, two-story houses, which were surrounded by large, tree-studded, green lawns. A general store, a public house, livery stable, and an occasional sawmill, or small warehouse marked the "business district" of these towns.

The grade became steeper as they approached the southern tip of Sebago Lake. Chabot was amazed at the size of the flat, gray sheet of water, rimmed by forests, with the hills of western Maine and New Hampshire marking the skyline. This lake could supply Portland with an endless amount of water by gravity flow with little or no pumping.

From the Lake, Henry turned westward toward the little crossroad village of Standish where he visited family friends. It was hard for the townspeople to realize that this prosperous businessman from California was formerly that wild, mischievous, little Henry Pierce.

The town's only "side street," a narrow dirt lane, led to two rival Congregational churches whose members had feuded about 30 years before. On the right side of the street, near the village, was a typical New England-style white church built by dissidents from a barn-red church a few hundred yards down the same side of the lane. Across the street, between the churches, irregular rows of white stones dotted a well-tended little graveyard. Next door to the red church, Henry turned his buggy into the drive of the white, two-story farmhouse of Betsy Hasty.

Betsy, a widow, was the mother of six children, half of whom were buried with their father under the straight row of identical thin, flatfaced, stones standing in the Hasty plot across the road. She still had one unmarried daughter, Ellen, at home.

Anthony, now a bachelor of fifty, was immediately attracted to the cheerful farm girl who was 20 years his junior. For him the visit to the Hasty household was much too short. As he drove with Henry down the Portland Road, it was difficult for the hydraulic engineer to keep his mind on the Portland water problem.[7]

When they presented their water proposal to Portland's authorities, Anthony and Henry were once again rebuffed. There had been previous plans to bring Sebago water to Portland and the idea had been turned down. Now a group of local entrepreneurs had already invited other East Coast capitalists with water experience to join them in forming a water company, which would be finally organized in 1866. There was no room for the West Coast duo.[8]

Chabot and Pierce visited Lynn, Massachusetts, the home of Henry's married sister, Ann. Here, Chabot seems to have invested in local enterprises, probably involving grain or other commodities. Marshall Pierce speculated in commodities, and it is likely that Henry and Anthony followed suit. Chabot still had investments in Massachusetts as late as the early 1870's. It is hard to imagine that Anthony did not somehow make money. But during his two-year stay in New England, his business involvements were not sufficiently significant to be a matter of public record. From that standpoint his eastern odyssey was a failure.[9]

On the other hand, Anthony's social life blossomed during this period. While he was in Lynn, Ann introduced him to many eligible spinsters. There were numerous unattached ladies at this time as most young men were away fighting in the Civil War. Although Anthony was then fifty, the shortage of younger men, plus his considerable wealth, made the shy little Frenchman quite the eligible bachelor.

He appears to have enjoyed meeting the young ladies of Lynn, but Anthony's heart remained in Standish. The plump, smiling, rosy-cheeked, country girl was always in his thoughts.[10]

Like many quiet, retiring men, Anthony was stubborn and persevering. As he jumped off the stage at Standish crossroads, his mind was made up. He was hopelessly in love, an emotion which he had never before encountered. Rehearsing in his mind what he wanted to say to Ellen and her mother, he walked briskly toward the lane which led to the Hasty home. Anthony mechanically tipped his hat to ladies he had met on his previous visit, but when Chabot was involved in deep thought, he recognized no one.

Speculation was soon rife in the small community on the purpose of this visit. Standish was a typical small village, though compared to most New England towns, it was quite young—only about 100 years old. First called Pearsontown, the hamlet later named itself after Miles Standish of Mayflower fame. One of its few distinctions occurred during the War of 1812. Portland had been attacked and burned by the British during the Revolution, and it feared a repeat peformance in the current conflict. So it quietly shipped all its gold by ox-cart to remote and inconspicuous Standish for safe keeping.[11]

The object of Anthony's visit was one of the oldest homes in the community, the 100-year-old Hasty house. Ellen's father, William, had been born there, and it was there he brought his bride, Betsy Fitch, from Baldwin. All six of the Hasty children were born in the beautiful family home. When William died in 1837, Betsy bought a cemetery plot that faced the road—in view of the Hasty house.

Betsy's last two children, Ellen and Emily, were twins, born on December 9, 1833. Emily married in the late 1850's and had two boys. Her husband, Daniel Comstock, a miner, had briefly

Anthony Chabot, Ellen Hasty, Marriage Photo, 1864.
(Steep Falls, Maine, Library.)

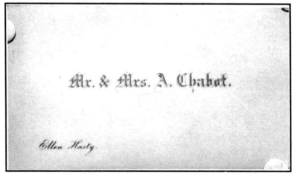

Calling card. (Steep Falls, Maine, Library.)

The "Red Church," built 1804, Standish, Maine, where Chabot and Ellen were married in 1864. The white house is said to be on the site of the Hasty homestead which burned in 1899. (Photo by Author.)

taken his family away from Standish in the early 1860's, and Emily may not have been present during Ellen's romance.

Chabot surprised the Pierces, and probably the Lynn ladies, when he announced his engagement. An impatient, restless man, Anthony wanted a short engagement, and Ellen agreed. The happy couple married in Standish on March 10, 1864, probably in the old red church next door to the house.[12]

Chabot seems to have reverted to using "Antoine" while in Maine and so registered his name on the marriage certificate. The large French-Canadian population in Maine made him comfortable with his French name, which he used off and on the rest of his life.

Shortly after Chabot's marriage Henry Pierce returned to San Francisco. It was obviously Chabot's intention to do the same, as he had listed San Francisco as his home on the wedding certificate. But he was comfortable in Standish, and he probably had to make short trips to attend to his investments. By the time he was ready to return, it was winter. He would not expose his beloved bride to the rigors of a winter overland trip, or the dangers of a sea voyage in Confederate-infested waters. They remained in Standish that winter.

But spring found Ellen pregnant. It would be another year before Ellen or her baby could travel. By this time Antoine must have been very restless, having had no major business enterprise for three years. But he would not consider leaving without Ellen. They had inscribed on their wedding photo, "Together we stand," and Anthony stood by Ellen during her pregnancy.

Ellen was never to see California. On Wednesday, October 18, 1865, she gave birth to a daughter in the house at Standish. She died in labor, but the baby lived. Anthony named his daughter after her mother—Ellen Hasty Chabot.[13]

The sorrowing family and friends carried Ellen across the road to the Hasty plot. A small, squat stone, unlike the other Hasty stones, was simply inscribed across the top, "Ellen Chabot," and temporarily marked Ellen's resting place.

Grief stricken, Chabot left the baby with her grandmother, and fled to San Francisco. In the white farmhouse in Standish, Betsy Hasty was joined by her surviving daughter, Emily, and Emily's husband and two boys. Helped, no doubt, by Chabot's money, this loving family raised baby Ellen in an idyllic, rural setting until she was almost five.[14]

CHAPTER 7

Discovers Oakland

Heartsick and discouraged Chabot arrived in San Francisco in late November, 1865. His usually vigorous stride was languid as he walked up Bush Street toward the Occidental Hotel. The last four years had not been happy ones. He had gone east confident of his ability to create new water systems. But Milwaukee and Portland had shown little interest in his hydraulic background. New York capitalists had practically laughed him out of town when he proposed connecting New York and Pennsylvania with an oil pipeline. He had, no doubt, made a few profitable investments in Maine and Massachusetts, but these were not hydraulic projects.

The only bright spot of his eastern trip, his marriage to Ellen, had turned into a tragedy. He had dreamed of disembarking at San Francisco with a beautiful bride and a baby daughter. But Ellen was in the Standish graveyard; his baby was with her family. Anthony was alone.

San Francisco had changed. New buildings were everywhere. The streets were full of strangers. Anthony was more depressed than he had been since he had walked those lonely streets in New York when he was a boy. He listlessly signed the register at the Occidental Hotel, a luxurious establishment at Montgomery and Bush, where he would live for over three years.

Only through working, through some active new enterprises, would Chabot shake his depression. Remi came to Anthony's new office on Montgomery Street near Jackson. He explained that the merger of the old Bensley Water Company with Spring

Valley Company had eliminated opportunities in water supply on the peninsula. Remi had been doing well in the sewer pipe field, but Anthony declined to join him. Chabot wanted to return to the water business.[1]

The office door opened and in bounded an old acquaintance, Joseph Eastland. Even at the age of 34, with his patrician nose and mustache and goatee, he looked like a typical "Kentucky Colonel." Joseph had served in the Mexican War as a clerk in the Quartermaster Corps under his father, an army major. At the end of the war, he traveled to San Francisco and worked in Peter Donahue's foundry. When Donahue established the San Francisco Gas Company, he appointed Eastland its secretary.[2]

In a high-powered monologue, Eastland explained his scheme for establishing a gas lighting company in Oakland. On December 9, he would be granted a franchise to produce and sell gas and to lay down pipes in the city of Oakland. Eastland was now organizing the Oakland Gas Light Company. Would Anthony join him and invest in one-third of the shares of the company?

Anthony scoffed. Oakland was a village of 1,500 people. It had no purpose except as a delightful, oak-shaded picnic and hunting ground for San Franciscans on Sundays. Joseph countered that during Chabot's recent absence Oakland's population had almost doubled, and in a very few years the city would be the terminus for the transcontinental railroad. Eastland stressed that someone was going to put gas lights in the streets and buildings of Oakland, and it was going to be Eastland.

To Anthony's argument that he knew nothing about a gas works, Joseph responded that an experienced gas producer, Henry Adams, would superintend the works. Before Chabot could respond, Eastland promised to make Anthony president of the company if he would invest. Anthony, restless and in search of a new project, agreed to cross the Bay to see what this village of Oakland might offer.

Chabot stood on the windy upper deck of the ferry as it plowed across the choppy bay. The screaming gulls circled overhead, and the giant side wheels splashed noisily. Anthony idly watched the rocking movement of the walking beam as the tall, black funnel belched sooty smoke that nearly hid Goat Island. He was again musing about his little freight boat on the Ohio when his thoughts were interrupted by the chatter of several young men carrying books. They explained that they were students at the College of California in Oakland. It was much quicker getting to school from San Francisco now that the ferry docked at Oakland Point on the Bay and no longer had to wind its way among the sandbars of San Antonio Creek to the Broadway dock. They also told him that the college was buying some land far out in the country near Strawberry Creek and might even become the state university.

As the ferry nosed into the busy wharf, Chabot could see an oak-covered plain, bounded by a ridge of barren, green hills on the east and the blue expanse of the Bay on the west. He was reflecting on how to store water in those hills during the rainy winters to supply the plain in the dry summers, as he was hustled off the boat and onto a steam train. The busy train quickly carried him down tree-lined Seventh Street, past elegant new homes, to the Broadway terminal.

Again Chabot was startled by the changes over the past few years. Broadway was now paved up to 14th Street, and an extension of Broadway led to a vast new cemetery at the foot of the hills. To the east, Twelfth Street crossed the old bridge over San Antonio Slough into the thriving suburbs of Brooklyn, Clinton, and San Antonio. Dr. Samuel Merritt was planning a dam that would soon convert the muddy slough into a beautiful lake. A new thoroughfare, Telegraph Road, followed the recently strung telegraph line north to Temescal Creek and then over the hills to Contra Costa County.

The busy downtown thoroughfares were lined with shops and businesses, and spacious homes were tucked among the oaks on the side streets. Antoine noticed that nearly every building had a well and a tank house with a windmill. Ground water was easily available. He also critically observed that many wells were very close to outhouses. The volunteer firemen depended entirely upon cisterns from which to pump water. Fortunately, there had been no major fires.[3]

The winter night had fallen before Chabot had completed his tour of Oakland. The businesses on Broadway had closed, leaving the street pitch black. From the ferry he could see the twinkling gaslights outline the streets of San Francisco. Yes, he would invest in Eastland's venture. Oakland could support a gas lighting system. But, he thought with much more enthusiasm, Oakland was also going to need a water supply system.

During the planning stages of the Oakland Gas Company in the spring of 1866, Chabot frequently visited Oakland. He became acquainted with the community and with its leading citizens, especially its political leaders whose cooperation he needed. The key figure in Oakland politics at that time was councilman Frank K. Shattuck who had been active in local politics and land development since 1852. Shattuck, who immediately recognized that both gaslights and a water supply would improve Oakland's property values, worked closely with Anthony, and the two men became lifelong friends.[4]

The Oakland Gas Light Company was incorporated on June 12, 1866 with $150,000 capitalization. Joseph Eastland, W.W. Beggs, and Anthony Chabot were incorporators. Anthony was elected first president. The trio wasted no time. A coal-gas plant was built on Washington Street between First and Second streets, and gas pipes were laid in the streets. Connections were made to 15 buildings, and to the first street light at Seventh and Broadway. On December 1 service was inaugurated. Business boomed and the company was an immediate success.

But Anthony's heart was not really in the gas venture. He knew nothing of gas manufacturing and realized that, aside from his activities on the Board of Directors, he could never be an active participant in the company's operations. Within a few months Chabot resigned as president. He was succeeded by H.H. Haight, who in 1867 would become Governor of California.[5]

Water was Anthony's first love. He soon convinced the politicians that a water supply system was as vital to Oakland's future as a gas company, and that he was the man to build the water works. During the spring of 1866, he studied the streams that flowed from the East Bay hills. Chabot was disappointed that most of the streams had small watersheds on the forward slopes of the hills with no sites for dams to store the winter rains. But he did find three streams whose watersheds were in longitudinal valleys behind the first range of hills and which entered the plain through steep canyons. These streams normally flowed year-round, and their canyons could be dammed to create sizable reservoirs in which to store the winter runoff.

The Frenchman's dark eyes flashed with excitement as he drove his buggy up the narrow, rutted county road through San Leandro Canyon about ten miles south of Oakland. A deep gorge was flanked by steep, tree-studded hills; yellow wildflowers waved in tall, green grass still wet from the spring rains. Raging San Leandro Creek, turgid with mud, fed by a vast watershed that stretched as far as the Moraga Valley, gushed from the canyon and poured across the plain into San Leandro Bay. Anthony recognized this creek with its year-round flow as the ideal source of Oakland's water supply. He visualized a great dam between these green hills and a sparkling reservoir that could supply the growing city for the foreseeable future. Although in 1866 he had neither the capital nor the time to supply Oakland from that source, Chabot would not forget his dream dam in San Leandro Canyon.

Anthony drove eastward up a straight road that led to the hills about three miles east of Oakland. He passed recently constructed, imposing homes set amid orchards of flowering fruit trees. Near the road Sausal Creek meandered through the shallow valley. The idyllic setting was aptly called Fruit Vale. At the foot of the hills the valley suddenly narrowed into a deep V-shaped canyon that cut through the first range of hills. Sausal Creek now tumbled wildly through this rocky gorge. Although its watershed was too small for a major reservoir, there were ample sites for a low dam that could be quickly and inexpensively constructed only five miles from Oakland. Chabot would keep this canyon in mind in case of emergency.

The third waterway, Temescal Creek, flowed westward across Telegraph Road about four miles north of Oakland. As he followed the rain-swollen creek toward the sodden, verdant hills, Anthony entered a wide ravine which turned southward into a U-shaped canyon behind the Oakland foothills. The creek's extensive watershed, generously supplemented by springs, covered most of today's Montclair District and provided the creek with a year-round flow. A modest dam across the U-shaped canyon would impound a large volume of water. The site was close to Oakland and, while the dam was under construction, the stream itself could be tapped near Telegraph Road and the water piped directly into the city. From this site Chabot could provide Oakland with water for the next decade, by which time he could have his giant San Leandro project completed![6]

But Chabot's dream was jolted when he learned that someone else had designs on Temescal Creek. While exploring the ravine leading to his dam site, Anthony was puzzled by a scene of devastation. He was later upset to learn that the jumble of mud and timbers marked the spots where two modest-sized dams under construction had been washed away by heavy rains in November, 1865. The site was on the ranch of Enoch Bidleman who had incorporated the Oakland and Alameda Water Company the previous September. Bidleman had a crew surveying the damage and was preparing to rebuild the dams. He had already petitioned the Oakland City Council for permission to lay pipes in Oakland and to supply the city with water. By May, 1866, Bidleman's new dams were underway, and he was ordering pipe. But his petition for a franchise had been pigeonholed in a City Council committee for many months.[7]

Although recently a rash of highly speculative water companies had been incorporated for land condemnation purposes, this fellow Bidleman was no speculator. He could present a serious threat to Chabot's plans. Anthony remembered only too well how George Ensign's little Spring Valley Company had swallowed the San Francisco City Water Works. The frowning little Frenchman vowed that there would be no repeat performance in the East Bay.

Anthony rushed back to San Francisco and met with his two associates with whom he had been planning his Oakland water project. His loyal brother, Remi, had assisted him with water projects in the gold country and in San Francisco and also had pipe making experience. Henry Pierce, Chabot's associate in his recent eastern venture, was an astute, if ruthless, business man, and had money to invest. On June 13, 1866, the day after the incorporation of the gas company, the three men incorporated the Contra Costa Water Company, with capital stock of $250,000, for the purpose of furnishing the cities and towns of Alameda County with pure, fresh water. Anthony subscribed to the majority of the shares and was duly elected president, and also appointed superintendent of the new company.[8]

Meanwhile, Chabot had been cultivating the members of the City Council, especially his friend, Frank Shattuck. Frank, who with Mayor-elect, John Dwinelle, had incorporated a speculative water company of his own, was chairman of the powerful Streets and Building Committee. It was in his committee that Bidleman's franchise petition had been pigeonholed. But Shattuck now decided that his own water project was impractical, and agreed to support his friend, Anthony.

On July 3 Chabot petitioned the City Council for the privilege of laying down pipes in the "streets, alleys, and lanes" of Oakland. Shattuck moved that the petition be referred to a special committee which he would chair, and which would include another friend of Chabot, E.P. Barstow. Within two weeks Chabot's franchise was granted.

The ordinance provided that the Contra Costa Water Company be granted a franchise to lay mains in Oakland for the purpose of supplying pure, fresh water to the inhabitants. The company was required, within 18 months, to lay 3,000 feet of pipe within the city limits and to supply water to all who agreed to pay for it as long as the supply permitted. The city was allowed to erect hydrants at its own expense and connect them to the mains. Chabot was disappointed when Shattuck was unable to railroad through an exclusive franchise for the Contra Costa Water Company. But the ordinance did provide that if any other company were granted better terms, those terms would also apply to the Chabot company.

When the Council meeting was about to adjourn, Anthony was stunned to hear a councilman weakly remind his colleagues

Anthony Chabot. (Steep Falls, Maine, Library.)

Remi Chabot. (Oakland Public Library, Oakland History Room.)

that the Oakland and Alameda Water Company had been waiting for a franchise for six months. So the Council awarded Bidleman's company a franchise on the same terms as Chabot's. The possibility of competition was a stimulant to Anthony. He

Henry Pierce. (Steep Falls, Maine, Library.)

became a whirlwind of activity.[9] Chabot's immediate problem was getting water from some source, any source, into Oakland within 18 months. He certainly could not get water rights and lands on Temescal Creek, build the large dam, and run pipes to Oakland within the allotted time. His short-range plan was to run pipes out Telegraph Avenue and tap water directly from the creek. But this idea could possibly be thwarted by Bidleman, whose ranch lay on the creek between Telegraph and the site of Chabot's proposed Temescal Dam. A long water rights battle between the rival companies could eat up the 18 months.

Therefore, Anthony turned to the closest alternative source of water. On July 30, 1866, he commenced legal proceedings to acquire land and water rights on Sausal Creek. Chabot announced plans to build a six-foot high dam at the lower end of present-day Dimond Canyon from which he would run about five miles of pipe into Oakland. By this scheme, Anthony could fulfill his franchise terms to supply Oakland within 18 months even if Bidleman did try to tie up Temescal Creek.[10]

Probably Anthony's threatened "end run" was not necessary. It appears that Bidleman had lost interest, or was financially unable to compete with Chabot, as he made no effort to interfere with Anthony's activities on Temescal Creek. Soon the Contra Costa Company temporarily abandoned its efforts on Sausal Creek and returned to its original game plan.

Anthony surveyed Telegraph Road where he planned to run a four-mile, six-inch main from Oakland to Temescal Creek. As this road was absolutely straight with a gradual, even rise in elevation, construction would not be difficult. The creek bed was 90 feet above the city which would provide a low, but adequate, pressure for Oakland's one-and two-story buildings. He ordered the pipe for this project and also the necessary 3,000 feet of mains for downtown Oakland, which he impatiently awaited. During the fall of 1866, Anthony established at the foot of Webster Street a company yard to store supplies and to serve as the Oakland office of the Contra Costa Water Company. Anthony's office at 728 Montgomery, in San Francisco, served as corporate head-quarters.

The pipe finally arrived at the Broadway wharf on December

1, 1866, and was stored and processed at the company yard. Chabot wasted no time. He immediately hired a crew of workmen, and, under his personal direction, ditches and piles of dirt soon disrupted Broadway. Within two weeks pipes had been laid from the wharf to Sixth Street, and by January the six-inch main to Temescal Creek had reached the junction of Broadway and Telegraph. But the January rains turned Telegraph Road into a quagmire and slowed the progress toward the Creek.[11]

Meanwhile, Chabot had been busy promoting his water company and signing up subscribers to his service. He even laid service pipes to his first customers—the Oakland Gas Company (in which he owned an interest), and Hutchinson's Nursery. He also erected a tap at Sixth and Broadway for the use of a street sprinkling wagon. But the pipes would remain empty, and no revenue would be realized, until the bogged-down main could reach Temescal.[12]

Then Anthony had an inspiration. Why not use well water until Temescal was reached? The College School, the preparatory school of the College of California, between Franklin and Webster, had a deep well from which water was pumped by a crochety windmill to a large, elevated tank. Surely those college boys did not need all that water! The Frenchman enthusiastically outlined his plan to Reverend I.H. Brayton, principal of the school. Chabot offered to supply the college with a strong, steam-powered pump to keep the water tank full if he could connect the tank to the water company mains. The scholarly schoolmaster could see the advantage of a good pump to replace the unreliable old windmill. And there was plenty of water for all.

By early April, 1867, less than nine months after his franchise had been granted, Anthony Chabot had laid his 3,000 feet of mains, and was supplying Oakland—actually only a few buildings on Broadway—with water. On May 1, the company published its first water rate schedule. The Contra Costa Water Company was in business!

Two weeks later, on May 14, Anthony received the first of thousands of complaints that his water company would receive over the next 40 years. No water was flowing from the taps! The students were thirstier than expected. This embarrassment occurred again on June 7. But the few customers, all businessmen and mostly Anthony's friends, were tolerant of the embryonic company's growing pains, and there were no storms of protest.[13]

Meanwhile, the rains having ceased, the water main was creeping up Telegraph Road. On May 1 Chabot secured a deed giving the company the right to divert water from the bed of Temescal Creek on the Alden ranch near Telegraph Road. Anthony beamed with satisfaction near the end of June when water from Temescal Creek reached Oakland and replaced the supply from the college.[14]

At first, leaking mains caused Chabot much irritation and expense as he watched his water spurting out of the street and flowing down the gutters. But his growing number of customers were unconcerned about the leaks and were quite satisfied with the water. It was the dry season, and despite the fact that there was no filtering device, the creek water was clear and sparkling. The *Oakland News* on July 13, 1867, reported:

"As the water is pure and beautifully clear, it is likely that no one is troubled [about the leaks] except the owner of the works who pays for the repairs."

But the water pressure proved to be inadequate even for Oakland's low buildings. Chabot soon corrected this problem by running his pipe up Temescal Creek about a mile above Alden's property to a new intake at a higher elevation. He then began building a brick and concrete million-gallon storage reservoir on Academy Hill (now "Hospital Hill") between Broadway and

Early advertisement in 1869 Oakland City Directory. (Oakland Public Library, Oakland History Room.)

Telegraph at 31st and Summit streets. This reservoir, completed in early 1868, was 100 feet above tide water, and provided Oakland with sufficient pressure for many years.[15]

During the remainder of 1867 and 1868 Chabot expanded his main system. By the end of 1867 most businesses and a few residences were served by the water company. But they were no longer happy customers. The winter rains turned the clear, sparkling creek into a muddy torrent. Anthony scowled on the morning of December 10, 1867, as he read in the *Daily Morning Journal*:

"The water obtained from the mains of the Contra Costa Water Company last evening was quite muddy and almost unfit for household purposes. Water from almost any well was superior."

Despite the complaints, by the end of 1867 Chabot had supplied Oakland with a tolerably good, though temporary, water system. Financially, he had certainly not made a fortune. His net profit that year from the water business was only $2,945. He was fortunate that the winters of 1866-67, 1867-68, and 1868-69 were exceptionally rainy, so that Temescal Creek could provide the few subscribers of the water company with a sufficient quantity, if not quality, of water while he constructed Temescal Dam.[16]

CHAPTER 8

Temescal Dam

Chabot had plunged into the preliminary work on Temescal Dam before his temporary system had been completed. He knew the community would soon gulp dry the trickle that flowed through the six-inch pipe from the creek. Oakland's rate of growth was greater than even its most fervent boosters had predicted. New businesses and residents were arriving daily, and the newcomers tended to subscribe to the company's water rather than dig wells and erect windmills. Anthony realized that before 1870, Oakland would hear the whistle of the first transcontinental train thundering toward the station at Broadway and Seventh. The city's population would then swell even more. He had to get that big dam built. And soon!

Anthony, in his quiet, unassuming manner, was a dynamo of energy. He was not only developing the Oakland water system, but simultaneously (as will be discussed later) he was involved in the first water company in San Jose, and by 1869 he was planning a dam in Vallejo. His brain seethed with ideas. He was so immersed in his plans for his projects that he often passed friends and acquaintances on the street without recognizing them. This trait was to amuse, and sometimes irritate, Chabot's friends for the rest of his life.[1]

Aside from his work, Anthony had little to fill his life. He frequently longed for his two-year-old daughter, Ellen, who was happily growing up on the farm at Standish. This little girl was a link to the happiest few months of his life. He desperately wanted her with him, but, despite his wealth, he alone could not provide her a suitable home. He was consumed with guilt when he corresponded with Mary Ann Bacheller, one of the spinsters he had met at Lynn, Massachusetts. His dear, dead wife, Ellen, was the only woman he could ever love, yet Mary Ann might provide him with a way to be near his beloved Ellen's little namesake.

Although Chabot had a wide range of business associates, many of them active in San Francisco society functions, Anthony had little interest in social, cultural, or church activities. Anthony and his brother, Remi, had always been close. But now Remi was courting an attractive young French lady, Emelie Padey, and had little time for his older brother outside of working hours. Early each morning the lonely little Frenchman, his head filled with the day's plans, and noticing no one, walked erectly and vigorously from the Occidental Hotel to the Oakland ferry, or to the San Jose train. He did not return until late evening.

While awaiting construction equipment and supplies for his dam, Anthony spent the summer and fall of 1867 running up and down Temescal Creek acquiring the necessary water rights and land for the project. He was armed with a legislative act of 1858 that gave water companies the right to appropriate lands for water supply purposes. Most landowners below the dam site deeded water rights to Chabot for the nominal consideration of one dollar. But in cases where he needed large tracts of valuable farmland for the dam and the reservoir, negotiations were not so easy. These ranchers, many of them Anthony's friends, did not oppose the project, but they were not going to give up their lands for a nominal dollar. In January, 1868, the Contra Costa Water Company started condemnation proceedings. The landowners agreed to accept the prices set by the court. At this time, Enoch Bidleman sold Chabot 31 acres of land for $1,000, thus effectively ending the rival Oakland and Alameda Water Company.[2]

Anthony gave the construction of the dam his constant supervision during 1868. Except for occasional trips to San Jose, he was at the dam site almost every day. At this time Henry Pierce was not active in the daily operations of the company, as he was frequently involved in the East, or in England, in his grain trading business.[3] Remi was busy in San Francisco manufacturing pipes for both the Contra Costa and the San Jose water companies. He later moved these activities to the corporation yard in Oakland. So in addition to constructing the dam, Chabot also had charge of the daily activities of the water company. To be closer to his work, Anthony moved from the Occidental Hotel in San Francisco to the Eureka Hotel at 7th and Washington streets in Oakland.[4]

As Anthony was not an engineer by education, he hired William Boardman, professional civil engineer and surveyor, to assist him with surveys and plans. Boardman first came to Oakland in 1857, and was a prominent and respected surveyor and engineer until his death in 1906. During the years 1865 to 1869, he was also City Engineer, and was the engineering adviser to the water company during the remainder of Chabot's life. Thus began a tumultuous relationship in which the self-educated, strong-willed Frenchman made almost all of the engineering decisions and expected the trained engineer to support those decisions by preparing the necessary drawings and written reports.[5]

Chabot located the dam in a 700-foot wide U-shaped canyon. There the south fork of Temescal Creek (which flows north from the present Montclair district) had its confluence with the east branch of the Creek (which roughly follows Highway 24 from the Caldecott Tunnel). He decided to place the dam across a relatively narrow spot in the canyon about 300 feet upstream from the present dam. This appeared to Chabot to be the logical site. Not only would the dam be relatively short, but two hills jutting out into the valley at that point would buttress the structure on each end. He quietly told Mr. Boardman, who was supposed to be the engineer, to make the detailed drawings for a dam at that location. Boardman objected. He had made test borings on the valley floor and had found no solid earth or rock for the dam's foundation at an economical depth under that area. Chabot was furious. His dark eyes flashed fire. His voice was calm but firm. He was paying for this project; he was paying his assistants; he was the superintendent; and he knew where he wanted the dam! Boardman shrugged and drew the plans for a dam at that site.

Every day Chabot impatiently paced the muddy canyon. He urged on his Chinese workers. After hacking away an old vegetable and potato garden, they began to dig the foundation for a puddle wall and to construct a masonry wasteway. The workers dug deeper each day as Anthony peered through his small wire-rimmed glasses into the excavation looking for some sign of bedrock. But to his disgust all he saw was muddy, porous soil. One day, many weeks and $15,000 later, Chabot abruptly ordered his crew to begin digging a few hundred feet farther downstream where Boardman's borings had indicated that bedrock was closer to the surface. Boardman smiled wryly, but wisely said nothing. He quietly returned to his drawing board and made plans for a new dam and wasteway. Anthony had made an expensive mistake![6]

Despite occasional clashes, and Chabot's occasional mistakes, Boardman respected the Frenchman. The engineer said in later years, "He [Chabot] was the man that told you where the dam would be built, and how he wanted it built, and he paid for it. An engineer would tell him what he thought he ought to do, but Mr. Chabot would tell him what he would have done. He was a man of excellent judgment. He was about as much of an engineer there as I was." [7]

At the new site, much to Boardman's satisfaction, bedrock was quickly reached. The bedrock upon which the dam would rest was scraped clean across the bottom and up the sides of the canyon. A total of 10,000 cubic yards of dirt was excavated. Meanwhile, clay was hauled by wagons from farther up the canyon and poured into the excavation. It was spread in thin layers, and each layer was wet down and thoroughly tamped or "puddled" by driving horses back and forth across the clay. When the pit was finally filled, the wagons continued to bring another 22,000 feet of the impervious material. This was layered and

Lake Temescal, Chabot's first dam. Note two opposing points of land jutting out into the lake below the dam. This was the site of the shorter dam first proposed by Chabot. (Bancroft Library.)

tamped until a solid clay wall, resting on bedrock and anchored against the sides of the canyon, rose high above the canyon floor. This puddle wall was 30 feet wide at the bottom and tapered to 18 feet at the top.[8]

While the puddle wall was being constructed, Anthony put his old mining experience to use. He planned and supervised the construction of over four miles of ditches and flumes from the dam site up the canyons to higher elevations where creeks were diverted into the system. When the puddle wall was completed, dirt and gravel were shoveled from the hillsides into the flumes and sluiced onto the wall. This was a much quicker and less expensive means of earth moving than the conventional horse and wagon. These flumes were kept in place for several years after the dam was in operation, and the structure was raised and strengthened each rainy season.

As the dam neared completion, its inner side was faced with stone to prevent erosion. Meanwhile, Chabot cut a wasteway through solid rock around the north end of the dam to divert the overflow back into the creek. A masonry weir was then constructed and equipped with regulating gates.[9]

In order to conduct the reservoir's water to the mains that led to the city, Anthony ran a large pipe through the base of the dam. This pipe was to be connected to the bottom of a fifty-foot high brick tower with intake gates at various heights to regulate the flow from the lake. But Anthony had made another mistake. He constructed the tower on unstable land near the site of the first dam. The expensive, ornate structure had just been completed when it was struck by a landslide. Chabot watched in dismay as his tower disintegrated into a pile of bricks. Again Mr. Boardman wisely said nothing.

Chabot could not take the time to construct another fancy tower. The reservoir was starting to fill and Oakland would soon need its water. Instead, he ordered that a simple standpipe, supported by a float that rose or fell with the water level, be connected with the outlet pipe. A strainer over the standpipe kept foreign matter from clogging the mains. Just below the dam the water was aerated in a large, wooden, aeration tank before it passed into the main which led to the storage reservoir on College Hill. Anthony could see no need for further purifi-

Lake Temescal, 1931. This lake would become one of Oakland's favorite re-creation areas. No longer a reservoir, it is now part of the East Bay Regional Park District. (Oakland Public Library, Oakland History Room.)

cation of the water.[10]

By mid-summer 1869, the dam was practically finished. Without fanfare Chabot opened the outlet valve and let water into the mains. Despite his mistakes, he had reason to be proud of this dam—his greatest engineering feat to date! The completed dam would be 105 feet high, 600 feet long, and 16 feet wide on top. It would back up a lake nearly a mile long with a capacity of 188,000,000 gallons. This monument to Chabot is still there, over 120 years later! No longer a source of drinking water, the lake is a community recreation and swimming center under the jurisdiction of the East Bay Regional Park District. Also during the disastrous Oakland fire of October 1991, fire-fighting helicopters used the waters of Lake Temescal to combat the conflagration.

In the first week of November, 1869, the first transcontinental passenger train whistled into Oakland. Chabot's "pure, fresh, mountain water" was flowing through the Contra Costa Water

Company mains which had recently been extended to the entire incorporated area of the city.[11]

Although Oakland, for the time being, had sufficient water, the community complained that the water was often muddy, and the rates were much too high.

Homes were not metered as they usually are today. The water rate was based on the number of square feet of ground surface covered by the dwelling, plus a charge for each story over one. For example, a workman's tiny dwelling of 600 square feet would be charged $1.75 per month, plus 25 cents for each additional story. A larger home of 1,200 square feet would pay a basic rate of $3.00 plus 25 cents for each additional story. But these basic rates were only the beginning. Subscribers were irritated by a long list of extra fees, ranging from 25 cents to a dollar, for such items as bath tubs, indoor water closets, hose connections, horses, and for each person in the household over five in number. Watering one's garden cost one cent per square yard of lawn and garden space. Commercial users had equally stiff schedules. Especially irritating were unannounced compliance inspections by company agents.[12]

Protests to these rates were heard in the screech of rusty windmills which pervaded the city as tanks were filled with well water— often polluted from nearby outhouses.

The company also drew public protests by charging the city $150 for each hydrant connection, although there was no charge to the city for water used by the fire department. By the end of 1870, there were only three hydrants in the city. When Chabot charged $40 a week for sprinkling Broadway between 4th and 9th streets, the contractor refused to pay it. So the people blamed the water company for the dust that blew in their faces.[13]

But Anthony justified the high water rates. As his company grew, his costs had spiraled upward. His rent expense rose when he moved the company's office from the company yard, at the foot of Webster Street, to the more conveniently located new Wilcox Building at the southwest corner of Broadway and Ninth Street. The company's water was piped into the new building in September, 1868. Anthony could now attest to the purity of his water by drinking it himself.

At the company yard, Chabot installed a pipe processing plant in which pipes were dipped into hot asphalt to prevent corrosion. This expensive installation, under Remi's supervision, ended the rash of leaky pipes that plagued the company. Remi also built costly new stables on Telegraph Road for the company's teams, relieving congestion at the pipe yard.[14]

A decision by the city in 1870 caused Anthony an unexpected expense. The water company had laid many miles of pipes in the city streets, had replaced defective mains with asphalted pipes, and in many cases had increased the size of the mains. Then the city decided to regrade its street system. In many places the regrading exposed the existing mains. This forced the protesting Chabot to replace much of the existing pipe system.[15]

Chabot's greatest expense was paying off the debt on the Temescal system. The dam alone cost over $300,000 dollars to build. This represented mostly borrowed money at high interest rates.

In 1868-69 it was touch-and-go for Chabot's company. Revenues for 1868 were only $6,373. Assuming an average water bill of $100 a year, the company had only 60 subscribers. The following year the income doubled, but this was still low compared to the company's huge investment over the past four years. However, revenues kept increasing as new residents and businesses flooded into Oakland, and subscribed to the company's service. In 1870 the Contra Costa Water Company was well enough established to increase its capital stock from $250,000 to

$1,500,000 and to attract new investment. Chabot's company had survived its growing pains.[16]

Anthony was growing restless. Office routine and handling complaints irritated him. His office clerks could do that. The dam was finished except for being heightened, which would take several years. Boardman should at least be able to handle that. And his brother, Remi, could oversee the day-to-day construction and maintenance. In early 1870, Chabot moved back to San Francisco from which he could more easily travel to his enterprises in San Jose and Vallejo, and still watch over Oakland.[17]

On March 26, 1870, Anthony took the day off to attend the wedding of his handsome young brother, and closest friend, Remi, at Notre Dame Catholic Church in San Francisco. With his full beard, wavy hair, and twinkling dark eyes, the tall, slim, personable 42-year-old Frenchman had a distinguished appearance.[18]

The bride was a beautiful, 21-year-old French girl, Emelie Padey. Her father, Martin Padey was born in Savoy, then under Sardinia, and her mother was French. Her parents were married at Lyons, France, where Emelie was born in February, 1849. The following year the little family sailed from France for San Francisco. Emelie, barely two years of age, made the tortuous crossing of the Isthmus of Panama on the back of a porter. She was well educated, talented, and possessed a strong, driving personality. Emelie soon became a leader in Oakland society. She was one of the founders of the Fabiola Hospital which was built on land that her brother-in-law, Anthony, donated.[19]

Anthony greatly admired Emelie and thoroughly approved of his brother's choice. He probably felt that she would complement his brother's usually placid personality. Remi had recently moved to Oakland and brought his bride to their first home in that city. On December 27, 1870, Henrietta, the first of Remi's four daughters, was born.[20]

Despite his intense involvement with three water companies, Chabot's thoughts turned inward to his own lonely life. He decided to marry Mary Ann Bacheller. But it was hardly a love match. He had recently had a tall obelisk erected in the Standish cemetery to supplement the tiny headstone on Ellen's grave. The monument was inscribed:

"My dear wife, mother, thine absence we deplore, thy kind and cheerful voice we hear no more. But in that land of peace and rest, we hope to meet thee among the blest."

These words, were certainly not composed by a happy bridegroom looking forward to embracing a second wife, but by a man honorably marrying a governess for his daughter.[21]

The summer of 1870, must have been unhappy for the Hasty family. The sad faces of Betsy, Emile, Daniel, and the two boys watched sorrowfully as Anthony drove up to the white farmhouse to claim his daughter. It must have been equally traumatic for little four-year-old Ellen. She was gently led away from the only family she had ever known by a man whom she had heard about, but who was a total stranger.

The somber wedding that took place at the Central Congregational Church in Lynn, Massachusetts, on July 28, 1870, was in stark contrast to that joyous, festive occasion in the red church in Standish six years before. The bride, 36, a native of Lynn, was a plain, thin-faced, woman, who apparently had no marriage prospects at home. Mary Ann was faced with a life in a faraway land with a husband who still mourned his first wife and whose only interest was his work. But the marriage gave her a purpose in life. As it was unlikely that she would have children of her own, she was delighted at the prospect of a stepdaughter. The frightened, bewildered, sad-eyed little girl quickly warmed to her new stepmother, and a friendship was established that would last the rest of Mary Ann's life.

The groom, 56, despite being president of two water companies, modestly recorded his occupation as "Superintendent" on the marriage license,[22] and could only think of getting back to his work. Anthony quickly hustled his little family aboard a westbound train from Boston. It was a long, hard, tiring trip involving many changes of trains, and took about a week. The recently completed transcontinental railroad still required much grading and was bumpy and slow. There was little time for a honeymoon. Anthony plunged back into his work. Exactly two weeks after the wedding, an Oakland paper quoted Chabot concerning the effects of street grading on the water pipes.[23] But despite his problems, the Frenchman was more content. He finally had his daughter near him.

After a brief stay in San Francisco, Chabot settled his family in Oakland, probably at the Eureka Hotel. This was just a block from Remi and Emelie's first residence at 7th and Broadway, though they soon moved to a home at 8th and Harrison where they lived for over ten years.[24] A coolness seemed to develop between the Chabot wives, whose personalities were poles apart. Mary Ann, retiring, almost a recluse, doting on Ellen, lived cooped-up in a hotel. She probably resented the vivacious, beautiful, aggressive, Emelie who lived an active life in a spacious home surrounded by her growing family. But this coolness did not extend to Anthony, whose affection for Remi, Emelie, and their four daughters never faded. Anthony occasionally even included Emelie in his business and philanthropic activities, which, no doubt, exacerbated the estrangement.[25]

But Chabot had little time to delve into domestic problems. He had three water companies which occupied his every waking moment.

CHAPTER 9

San Jose & Vallejo

S eething with restless energy, Anthony, in the fall of 1866, was impatiently awaiting equipment and supplies to start the first phase of his Oakland water project. Lulls in his activities always irritated the water man. At that critical time Chabot met Donald McKenzie, a man of similar temperament and interests, from San Jose.

McKenzie was heir to a Scottish earldom, and his wife was a direct descendant of the Stuart line of English monarchs. Born in Glasgow, Scotland, he had first worked, at the age of 14, as a smelter in New Jersey before coming to California in 1850. Two

Donald McKenzie, founder, San Jose Water Company. ("Nine Men...," San Jose Water Company, Publishers.)

years later, in partnership with John Bonner, he established an iron works near First and San Antonio streets in San Jose.

Fascinated by McKenzie's Scottish brogue, Anthony learned about San Jose's potential. The community was founded on the east bank of the Guadalupe River in November, 1777, as the first *pueblo*, or civilian community, in California. Anthony's interest was sparked when he learned that the first activity of the 68 new settlers was to build a dam across the river for irrigation and domestic purposes. But the town grew very slowly and had a poor reputation during the Hispanic era. Even in 1849-1850, when San Jose was the first state capital under the American flag, the legislature was called, "the legislature of one thousand drinks." The capital was hastily moved to the pristine hills of Vallejo.

With the coming of American settlers in the 1850's, the lush Santa Clara valley filled with farms and ranches. San Jose merchants shipped the valley's produce to San Francisco through the port of Alviso. San Jose was soon a growing commercial center. In early 1864, the newly completed railroad to San Francisco condensed a nine-hour stage ride into less than two hours on the train. By 1866, San Jose, with nearly 9,000 population, was somewhat larger than Oakland.[1]

But McKenzie explained that water for domestic use was becoming a problem. Until the mid-1850's, settlers had carried water by hand from the *acequia*, a canal near Canoas Creek built during the Hispanic era. It roughly followed Almaden Avenue from an old dam near Virginia Street. This practice resulted in cholera and typhoid. In October, 1851, the Common Council had appointed a committee to investigate the problem. After deliberating the weighty situation for almost three years, the committee reported that redwood pipes should be run from the *acequia* to the fire department's cisterns that were scattered about the city. But no action was taken on the report.[2]

This inaction was possibly due to the fact that early in 1854 the Merritt brothers decided to dig a well on their property on Fifth Street. They struck water at 50 feet but decided to dig deeper. At 80 feet the water gushed up the well and into the air. The brothers found that the artesian water was tasty and plentiful. By late summer there were 40 or 50 artesian wells, most of them flowing uncontained. One such well shot water nine feet into the air and flooded nearby dirt streets to a depth of six inches. This well was a local tourist attraction, but it caused both the city and state governments to put severe restrictions, backed by heavy penalties, on uncontrolled artesian wells. The use of these wells diminished, and most householders were without pure water.[3]

Meanwhile, McKenzie had dug artesian wells to supply his foundry. In June, 1864, he obtained city permission to erect two large, elevated tanks into which he pumped artesian water. In

McKenzie's water tanks, present First and San Antonio Streets, 1866. (San Jose Water Company, Sharon Whaley, Public Relations Department.)

return, he agreed to supply the fire cisterns from this source. McKenzie's twin wooden tanks, totaling 100,000-gallon capacity, atop a 50-foot, wood-braced platform, looked down on the low buildings of the city and dominated the town's "skyline." With many of his neighbors using impure water from shallow wells or from the *acequia*, McKenzie saw a community need that he could fill and also make a tidy profit.

In February, 1865, the Scotsman obtained a 25-year franchise from the city council to supply "good and pure" water to the city's inhabitants at rates set by the council. The city reserved the right to buy the system at the expiration of the franchise. He soon laid pipes from his bulging water tanks to a number of homes. The new subscribers had plenty of water pressure. These tanks likely gave Chabot the idea of supplying his Oakland subscribers with water from the college water tank while his main was being extended to Temescal Creek.[4]

The San Jose water man suggested to his Oakland counterpart that they form a water company. Business was so brisk, that he would like to dig more artesian wells, and supply all of San Jose. But he needed the capital and the expertise of a man like Chabot. After a pleasant train ride past the prosperous farms and small towns on the San Francisco Peninsula, Chabot inspected McKenzie's facilities, verified the growth of the city, and agreed to join the Scotsman in a water company.

The San Jose Water Company was organized on November 26, 1866, by Donald McKenzie, John Bonner, Anthony Chabot, and Peter Carter with a capitalization of $100,000. McKenzie was elected president and William Rankin was appointed secretary. Unlike Chabot's ventures in San Francisco and Oakland in which he actively supervised the actual construction of the water works, his role in the San Jose Water Company was that of an investor, planner, and advisor. In San Jose the bespectacled, little Frenchman was not seen in rain gear and hip boots personally supervising the construction of a dam or a flume. Soon after Anthony joined the San Jose company, supplies arrived for his Oakland venture which occupied an increasing amount of his time during the next two years.

The new company soon laid water mains and supplied a growing number of subscribers with pure artesian water. But as the population grew, and the use of home wells diminished, still more demands were made on the San Jose Water Company. The output of the wells was soon insufficent to supply the booming city. Chabot and his cohorts realized that they would have to find a new source of water.[5]

Anthony and his colleagues decided that they should appropriate land and water rights on the upper reaches of Los Gatos Creek where there was a plentiful supply of pure water. Chabot recalled his Lobos Creek system in San Francisco. He envisioned a similar flume conducting the waters of Los Gatos Creek to a receiving reservoir nearer to town from which the water would be pumped through pipes into the city. On October 1, 1868, the San Jose Water Company petitioned in court for permission to condemn lands and water rights on Los Gatos and Campbell Creeks. This was soon followed with a series of water right acquisitions in which most owners settled for a nominal one dollar and for the right to tap the pipes that crossed their lands.

The key to the proposed system was the old Forbes Flour Mill, renamed the Los Gatos Manufacturing Company, in Los Gatos. From a small dam above the mill, at present Main Street and College Avenue, water was conveyed to the mill to run its machinery. The water company board and the mill owners agreed that the water company could take water into a flume from the mill's tail race. The flume would carry the water about two miles to a receiving reservoir, later known as Seven Mile Reservoir, from which it would be pumped through pipes to San Jose.

But it immediately became evident to the founders of the San Jose Water Company that the corporation was grossly undercapitalized for such a venture. In early December the trustees reorganized the company and increased its authorized capitalization to $300,000. But the original investors could afford no further contributions to capital. McKenzie and Bonner had their money in the iron works. Chabot was building an expensive dam in the Oakland hills. The trustees had to look elsewhere for money! [6]

Nathaniel H.A. Mason, a native of Tennessee, who had owned a water company in Stanislaus County, became interested in the venture and offered to supply a substantial share of the needed capital. But he drove a hard bargain. He demanded, and received, the presidency and control of the company. McKenzie was relegated to vice president, and Chabot, whose technical background and capital were still needed, was kept on an expanded board of trustees. All other officers and board members were new. The corporate "takeover" was effective on May 21, 1869. [7]

The new regime immediately put the plans of the old company into action, and added a few ideas of its own. In early August construction started on the two-mile flume from the flour mill toward the site of a 2,500,000-gallon reservoir about seven miles from San Jose on present Bascom Avenue. Work was also commenced on another reservoir about three miles from San Jose. A small impounding reservoir, Tisdale Reservoir, near Los Gatos, was jointly built by the water company and the milling company to add more volume to the system. Seven Mile and Three Mile reservoirs were connected by 13-inch pipe to San Jose and by seven-inch pipe to Santa Clara.

Mason was efficient! By 1871 the system was complete. It was expensive, though, and the trustees levied a total assessment of $96,000 on the shareholders to pay the cost. There must have been quite a stockholder uproar! But in June, 1872, it was quieted when the company's first dividend, one-half of a percent, was declared.[8] And Anthony did not do so badly. Those long water mains were fabricated by brother Remi in the Contra Costa Water Company's pipeyard in Oakland.[9]

Between 1874 and 1876 Anthony had no time for San Jose. He was busy on San Leandro Creek building a large reservoir which was later named Lake Chabot. And during those same years, the San Jose Water Company, under yet another president, was constructing its first major impounding reservoir in the hills above Saratoga. The reservoir was named Lake McKenzie. This was the first of many reservoirs that would eventually dot the hills above San Jose.[10]

Chabot lost interest in the San Jose company. He retired from its board and sold his stock. He was too involved in Oakland to give the company his active participation. Also, the San Jose Water Company was in the hands of very capable men who really didn't need Anthony's assistance.

Back in 1869, Anthony was again restlessly searching for a new venture. Temescal Dam was almost completed, and, for the time being, the Contra Costa Water Company offered its president no real challenges. In San Jose the water company had been taken over by Mason, and Chabot had been relegated to a back seat.

By this time Chabot's expertise as a water company developer was becoming well known in the Bay Area. He was contacted by Joseph Collins Edgcumbe, a young Vallejo contractor, who was interested in establishing a permanent water system in his town. Edgcumbe, like Chabot, was Canadian, although he was of English descent. He was born in 1838 in Cobourg on Lake Ontario and came to California at age 24. After working in the mines for a year, Edgcumbe settled in Vallejo where he became a contractor and builder.[11]

At first Anthony hesitated. Vallejo was unlike San Jose. It was a much smaller, younger city. In 1850, Mariano Vallejo, the former commandant of the Mexican outpost of Sonoma, owned

Joseph Edgcumbe, Chabot's associate, Vallejo City Water Company. (Vallejo Naval and Historical Museum.)

the site of the future city. His cattle and horses grazed on the wild oats that covered the rolling hills. Learning of the dissatisfaction with San Jose as state capital, Vallejo offered 156 acres of land, and pledged $370,000 toward a building fund, if the state moved its capital to his land opposite Mare Island. His offer was accepted.

The capitol building was completed in May, 1852. But even though it had a saloon in the basement, the legislators were not happy. There were few amenities in the tiny community nestled in the flat lands near the Napa River. The peripatetic legislature soon looked elsewhere for more congenial surroundings.

When the state government officials moved out, most of the townspeople left with them. In 1854 there were only a few scattered buildings between the Napa River and Sonoma Street, and Virginia and Pennsylvania streets. Over the next decade Vallejo grew slowly by fits and starts. It was not until the mid-1860's that the town showed much sign of life. A projected rail line to the Fairfield-Suisun area stimulated the city's growth. Anthony Chabot saw a future for the little town of 6,000 population, if it had a reliable water supply.[12]

Vallejo had the same situation that Chabot had so often seen in other small, growing towns—backyard wells with brackish, hard water, often polluted by outhouses. Some homes had cisterns to catch the winter rains. But by late summer, as one observer noted, "...the cisterns became lively from animalcula...." Other citizens bought water by the barrel at outrageous prices. To add to the problem, the householders became very upset about the lack of water in the dry summers, but lapsed into apathy during

Vallejo, 1869. Late that year "Anthony Chabot dropped quietly into town," and Vallejo soon had a water supply. (Vallejo Naval and Historical Museum.)

the rainy season.[13]

There was a plethora of proposed water companies. Most of them existed only on paper and lacked the capital and the engineering expertise to carry out their plans. Only one company, the Vallejo Water Company, seemed to be getting off the ground. That firm had incorporated in 1867 with the object of taking water from Sulphur Springs Creek (now Blue Rock Springs Creek), and from American Canyon Creek. In late 1869, the company publicly offered $25,000 worth of stock at ten dollars a share in four, easy, monthly installments. It was granted a franchise and in early January broke ground for a reservoir on Capitol Hill. It rashly promised water for the city by May. But the promoters were short of cash and the stock subscriptions were slow.[14]

About this time, as one reporter wrote, "Anthony Chabot dropped quietly into town." Anthony conferred with Edgcumbe. With little publicity, Chabot soon shipped pipe to Vallejo. In January he incorporated the Vallejo City Water Company, which was granted a 20-year franchise. Anthony was president and Edgcumbe was superintendent. Chabot announced that he would supply water to Vallejo within 12 months. That would mean a tight schedule.

During the first months of 1870 Vallejo had two active water companies each promising to supply the city with pure, fresh water. A third company also tried unsuccessfully to join the fray. The Vallejo Water Company advertised frantically for investors. It claimed to have made its surveys and cost estimates, and that it was ready to let contracts. To show its good faith, it continued to dig the Capitol Hill reservoir with a crew of seven or eight men, and promised to lay pipes at an early date. The company dangled a projected 25- to 30-percent return on cost. But investors were reluctant to bite. By the end of spring the old company threw in the towel.[15]

Meanwhile, the retiring little Frenchman was busily making surveys of his own. He found a site three miles north of the city where Blue Rock Springs Creek flowed through a U-shaped canyon. There he decided to build an impounding reservoir to assure year-round supply from an elevation that would provide adequate pressure to most of the city. The creek originated from underground springs (near Columbus Parkway), and also was fed by an estimated 5,000-acre catchment area.[16]

Once the site was selected, Chabot and Edgcumbe embarked on a crash program to meet their announced one-year deadline. Chabot purchased 425 acres of land in the canyon for $42,000, and Edgcumbe immediately started work on the dam. At the same time he began laying a 12-inch main toward the center of town, and also laid distribution mains in the streets. In July Chabot established a pipe manufacturing plant in Vallejo that could turn out 1,000 feet of pipe per week. A company office was estab-

Lake Chabot, Vallejo, ca. 1987. Today the shores are shared by a city park and Marine World, USA. (Photo by Author).

lished at Maine and Marin streets. This activity discouraged any embryonic water companies from hatching.[17]

The Vallejo project was expensive. To attract more capital the company increased its capital stock. But there was little investor interest. When Chabot came from San Francisco, often on Sundays, to inspect the works, he frequently carried bags each containing $1,000 in silver to meet operating expenses.[18]

By the end of 1870 the dam was almost completed and, aided by the winter rains, began to back up a substantial lake. The earthen dam was 300 feet in length and 40 feet high. (This was about half the length and one-third the height of Temescal.) When filled it formed an attractive, curved lake of about 100 acres, and, it was claimed, that it could supply Vallejo with 3,000,000 gallons per day. Chabot stocked his new reservoir with perch, and local citizens enjoyed fishing from the sunny banks of the reservoir. The reservoir is still called Lake Chabot, and a city park and Marine World Africa, U.S.A. share its shores.[19]

On December fifth the water from the reservoir reached the city. The pipes were checked for leaks. Numerous repairs were made and the system was thoroughly flushed while the community impatiently waited. In early January Chabot's first Vallejo customers turned on their taps. At first the water had a sulphur taste from the springs up the creek. But as rains diluted the stream, the taste disappeared.[20]

Anthony was now involved in three water companies. So, why not a fourth? He became interested in the prosperous river port of Napa. The town of 3,800 people needed water, and Chabot and a friend from Oakland decided to fill the need. In September, 1870, they incorporated the Napa City Water Company. But Anthony was overextending even his own inexhaustible energy. Vallejo was not going too smoothly, serious problems were developing in Oakland, and he still was involved in San Jose. As a result, Chabot was never active in Napa, and other entrepreneurs built Napa's water system.[21]

At first Vallejo's citizens were pleased with their new water works. Without it the future of the town would have been seriously handicapped. The ever-present danger of fire was alleviated by 35 fire hydrants connected to Chabot's system. But Anthony soon ran into problems. Complaints were heard that the price was too high and the service subject to interruptions. The company was still having trouble raising capital, and was unable to pay a dividend before 1874.[22]

About this time Anthony received a frantic message from Edgcumbe. The pipes were springing leaks throughout the system! When the Frenchman stepped off the boat, he could see puddles in the otherwise dusty streets. Geysers spurted from the main leading from the reservoir. Rivulets of mud flowed down the hillsides. Chabot was puzzled. He had successfully used riveted, sheet-iron pipes in other water ventures. But apparently chemical conditions in the Vallejo area soil caused them to rust through and leak. To make matters worse, there seems to have been no valve installed at the dam's outlet pipe. In a few weeks the entire contents of the lake had drained through the fissures in the pipes. For the remainder of the hot summer and fall the city was without piped water. Old wells and cisterns were put back into use; water carts went door-to-door selling water by the bucket or the barrel; and barges brought water from the Sacramento and San Joaquin rivers. Chabot replaced the sheet-iron pipes with cast iron-pipes. The system was restored. But the townspeople never forgot the incident, especially a stationer named John Frey who started a crusade for a municipally-owned water works.[23]

In late 1875 Chabot tried to redeem himself by completing the reservoir on Capitol Hill, which had been begun by the old

Vallejo Water Company. This reservoir (at 720 Capitol Street) was 150 feet above sea level. It fed the more elevated sections of the expanding city which were above the pressure level of the main reservoir. This ended pressure problems and the need for wells in the higher sections of the city.[24]

Anthony extended his system to Mare Island in 1876. In the early 1850's a civilian-operated drydock was established on the island. The water from old wells dug by early squatters caused illness, and water was shipped from Sausalito at two cents a gallon. In 1854 the Navy took over the island under Admiral Farragut of later Civil War fame. He dug new wells and built cisterns. In 1875 a small catchment reservoir was built near the south end of the island by placing an earth dam across a small ravine. But the island still had a water shortage.

Chabot laid across the Napa River a 2,000-foot cast-iron pipe with flexible joints that would follow the contour of the river bottom. He supplied the Navy installation with about 1,000,000 gallons per month, unless there was a severe water shortage. But frequently during the 1880's the pipeline ran dry, and the islanders had to rely on their own wells and little reservoir.[25]

Relations between the water company and Vallejo became increasingly bitter in the 1880's. It was evident that the Chabot company did not have the water resources to supply the growing area. Water shortages, and occasional outages, became more frequent. And, more important, the company indicated that it did not intend to expand its system to new sources. After Anthony's death in 1888, the company took a "take it or leave it" attitude toward subscriber complaints. In 1891 the city refused to renew the company's franchise.[26]

John Frey's campaign for a publicly-owned water supply attracted many supporters. Frey dwelt not only on the shortage of water but also on the impurity of the drainage from the barnyards along Blue Rock Springs Creek. After one unsuccessful try, Frey's group pushed through a bond issue in 1892 for the construction of a municipal system. The public system built its . first reservoir in Wild Horse Canyon, 21 miles away. Water was delivered in January, 1894. For a few years Chabot's old system continued to serve peripheral areas of the community and then went out of business.[27]

CHAPTER 10

Thirsty Oakland

Although Chabot, as we have seen, had water activities in other cities, his chief concern during the 1870's was the Contra Costa Water Company in Oakland. Through his own boundless energy and dogged determination, Anthony Chabot, practically single-handed, laid the foundations of Oakland's water system. It was in Oakland that he rose to prominence and made most of his money, much of which he returned to his adopted city through his philanthropy.

Demand for Contra Costa water soared during the 1870's. The population rose from 10,000 in 1869, when Temescal Dam

Oakland, 12th Street, 1869—about the time Chabot completed Temescal Reservoir. (Oakland Public Library, Oakland History Room.)

was completed, to 15,000 by 1873. By mid-decade 25,000 people were living in Oakland. Chabot not only supplied water to the farthest corners of Oakland, but, in October, 1870, he extended his service across Lake Merritt to the newly incorporated town of Brooklyn. This town, which was annexed to Oakland about two years later, extended southeastward about a mile to 14th Avenue. The ever-increasing population, coupled with a dry winter in 1870-71, made it apparent that, even before the dam was raised to its full height, Lake Temescal by itself would be inadequate to supply the community.[1]

Chabot's long-range solution to the problem was to construct the dam, which had long been his dream, on San Leandro Creek. From 1870 to 1876 this dam was his *raison d' être*.

As he became increasingly immersed in the San Leandro project, Chabot found it necessary to allow much of the internal operations of the Contra Costa Water Company to fall on others. He had the full cooperation of Remi who became, in fact, superintendent. Remi kept the Temescal system in operation, while Anthony handled the San Leandro undertaking.

But vice-president Henry Pierce, who previously had been mainly concerned with his grain business, now began to take an active interest in the water company's office operations. He moved the office to luxurious new quarters, at 458 Eighth Street, and installed his brother, Marshall, who had gone bankrupt in Maine, as cashier and treasurer. Marshall's son, Orestes, and son-in-law, H.T. Watkinson, later joined the company.[2]

Public relations became increasingly bitter as the new office staff took over, and Chabot spent more time in San Leandro. Rate complaints were quashed with the response that if the customer didn't like the rates, he could get his water elsewhere. Often the complaining householder found his bill higher the next month.

Anthony had strong humanitarian feelings, although he was

not above financial scheming, as was common in that era. He paid his workers the highest going wage and disliked having to fire a person, even for cause. He often tried to find jobs in other firms for his discharged employees. Chabot was once accused of political discrimination, but he indignantly replied that he had never fired a man because the employee had voted for the Democratic party.

Although Anthony's influence still ameliorated the worst public abuses, he was afraid that ruthless elements might take over his company. The *Oakland Daily News* commented, in 1874, that Chabot was liberal in his attitude toward people, but that he feared that an opposite type of character might step into his shoes and extort the people. His fears were well founded![3]

During the years that Chabot planned, financed, and constructed his dream dam on San Leandro Creek, Oakland teetered on the brink of a disasterous water shortage. Anthony often found it necessary to restrict public use of water and to apply inadequate "band-aid" solutions when shortages loomed. As a result, he was frequently reviled by the public and the press.

In the winter of 1870-71, in addition to raising the height of Temescal, Chabot began doing what old-time Oakland residents had done long before there was a water company. He started digging wells. Chabot ordered the drilling of several deep shafts, most of them east of Brooklyn where the ground water rose within a few feet from the top of the wells. Pumping was relatively inexpensive. These wells were soon adding 15,000 to 20,000 gallons per hour to the supply. Most of this water was pumped directly into the Brooklyn mains. But residents complained that the pressure was irregular, and that several wells were too close to slaughter houses. At least the subscribers had sufficient water. That was Chabot's legal obligation! But he realized that to continue to fulfill his obligation, he needed still another source of water before the dry season of 1872.[4]

Sausal Creek, which flowed from Dimond Canyon above Fruit Vale (Fruitvale), had attracted Anthony's attention back in 1866, before he started on Temescal. He had even commenced condemnation proceedings, but he had abandoned Sausal Creek and concentrated on the Temescal project. About 1870 Anthony watched with mixed feelings the progress of a new company, Caspar T. Hopkins' Sausal Water Company. Although this company was established to serve Fruit Vale residents, its franchise allowed it to lay pipes down Fruit Vale Road to present East 14th Street and into Brooklyn.

Caspar Hopkins, a well-known Bay Area insurance magnate, had a magnificent six-acre estate, Alderwood, on Sausal Creek in the present Dimond District. Hopkins had constructed a small stone dam in the upper part of the canyon and a distributing reservoir on a bluff just west of his estate. The million-gallon reservoir, at 325-feet elevation, could supply Brooklyn with abundant fresh mountain water with a strong, even pressure. While Hopkins could give Chabot serious competition, Anthony also saw the possibility of getting a ready-made water system for very little cost. He knew that Hopkins, between his estate and his water company, had seriously overextended himself. The Sausal Company was short of cash, and the shrewd little Frenchman doubted if Hopkins could get his mains to Brooklyn.

Chabot quietly, albeit nervously, watched and waited as his would-be competitor's pipes crept down Fruit Vale Road toward East 14th Street and then turned westward toward Brooklyn. By April, 1872, the Temescal supply, despite the winter rains, was dropping rapidly. Hopkins' reservoir was brimming over. Anthony would have to make a deal—but the longer he could wait, the better. Suddenly, work stopped on Hopkins' main, a mile short of his goal![5]

Anthony drove through the winding, tree-lined driveway of Alderwood. Rustic bridges crossed Sausal Creek which rushed to waste itself in the bay. On the wide porch of the large, low, Gothic-style cottage, under the alders, Caspar Hopkins patiently waited. After brief, unrecorded, negotiations, the grave little Frenchman drove back down the driveway. He glanced at the creek. A smile crossed his face. Most of that water was now his, and he needed it badly. Within ten days after the buy-out, Chabot had forty men busily extending Hopkins' pipes to the Contra Costa mains only a mile away in Brooklyn.[6]

Anthony then took a bold step. He shut off the main from Temescal. From the reservoir behind Fruit Vale he supplied the entire Oakland-Brooklyn area until mid-summer, 1872, allowing Lake Temescal to fill up. Then when the Fruit Vale system went dry, the Temescal system took over for the remainder of the dry season. Fortunately, the rains were early and exceptionally heavy that fall. Anthony breathed easier. He had again saved the day, at least for the time being.

As the heavy rains continued into January, Temescal and Sausal reservoirs began to fill rapidly. In February the *Daily Transcript* reported that "Our Water King, Mr. Chabot," had stated that the reservoirs were filled and that even if no more rain fell, the supply of water was adequate until the next rainy season. But "Our Water King" was a bit overly optimistic. The rains did suddenly stop. Chabot had misjudged the supply in the reservoirs and the thirst of the 15,000 Oaklanders.[7]

The Temescal system was designed for a 10,000 population. The wells and the Sausal system could not quite make up the difference. To make matters worse, the dry spring caused an early use of water for irrigating purposes. Oakland was a city of homes whose owners were proud of their lovely lawns and gardens. Furthermore, the homeowner paid a flat rate for water to irrigate his property and, consequently, he could see no reason why his sprinklers should not run all night.[8]

By May, 1873, the levels of the reservoirs were precariously low. The excessive waste of water dropped the level in the distributing reservoir on College Hill (Hospital Hill) so low that subscribers in the higher elevations of the city had almost no pressure. Customers were urged to stop wasting water, and in July the water company prohibited the use of stationary sprinklers. This order, though justified, did not build goodwill for Mr. Chabot and his water company.

Our frantic Frenchman next asked the city council to stop street sprinkling, or to use salt water. The disgruntled citizens watched their lawns turn brown and the dust rise in clouds from the streets. Rumors were again spread that the artesian wells in Brooklyn were surrounded by slaughter houses, and that the water was impure. One newspaper charged that the system was monopolized by one man, and that it should be regulated in the public interest. It urged that citizens dig their own wells. But despite the attacks, the Contra Costa Water Company continued to gain customers. The days of private wells were slowly drawing to a close.[9]

The water shortage inevitably raised the specter of a major conflagration. A scanty number of fire hydrants, low water pressure, and a not too efficient fire department made this danger very real. The City Council considered the idea of running a 12-inch pipe directly from Lake Temescal to the city hydrant system. This would give the fire system excellent pressure. The beleaguered Mr. Chabot tried to raise his popularity rating by endorsing the idea. He offered to pay 60% of the cost of the project, and, in addition, provide the water at no cost. But the indecisive City Council pigeonholed the proposal in committee.

In September a fire broke out in the McClure Military Academy which was located just below the distributing reservoir. A combination of low water pressure and firemen who could not find the hydrants proved a bit disastrous to the academy. Had the council acted promptly on Chabot's offer, the high pressure system could have been installed in time to prevent the disaster. But the public, still bemoaning their dried-up lawns, roundly condemned Chabot.[10]

Fortunately, the rains fell early and heavily in the fall of 1873. Eight inches of rain by the end of the year took public pressure off the harassed "Water King." Anthony was busy hauling supplies and equipment down the muddy county road (East 14th Street) toward San Leandro Canyon. He had to get started on that dam![11]

Chabot's enthusiasm for a dam on San Leandro Creek was well justified. In the first place, it was the largest creek within a reasonable distance of Oakland. Its watershed area of nearly 50 square miles, at least 14 times greater than that of Temescal Creek, provided a perennial flow even in dry years. The light, gradual fall of the lower section of the Creek permitted a large area to be flooded by a dam of reasonable height. Anthony chose for the site of his dam a narrow gorge less than 500 feet wide between two high hills. Close by the site there was plenty of clay for the puddle wall and rock for the masonry work. The *Canadien* amateur engineer worked out the details of his grand project, and gave them to his ever patient professional engineer, William Boardman, to draw up. If the rains would cooperate, he would bring water into Oakland by 1875.[12]

Anthony Chabot, the altruistic self-made water man, was planning to save Oakland from drought by supplying it with sufficient water for decades to come. But at the same time Anthony Chabot, the less-than-altruistic financier, was scheming to make himself a wealthier man.

He had heard how the "Big Four," Crocker, Huntington,

Stanford, and Hopkins, had incorporated the Central Pacific Railroad. They retained a controlling interest in the railroad but sold a large amount of stock to the public. The foursome then formed a closely-held construction company, the Crocker Company. As directors of the Central Pacific, they awarded contracts to the Crocker Company at exorbitant prices. To oversimplify, the equity of the railroad's stockholders was milked, while the Big Four became millionaires through their Crocker Company. Anthony was not yet a millionaire, but this was his chance!

In August, 1873, Anthony Chabot, the president and controlling stockholder of the Contra Costa Water Company, organized his own "Crocker Company," the California Water Company. Chabot's creation had a capitalization of $1,500,000, divided into 15,000 shares at $100 per share.

He was joined in the venture by E.M. Hall, D.P. Barstow, S. Huff, and William Haslehurst. The latter two men were large landowners on San Leandro Creek below the site of the proposed dam. Chabot subscribed to only 1,000 shares of stock for which he paid $10,000, or ten cents on the dollar of the stock's par value. The other incorporators each purchased 100 shares of stock for $1,000. Thus Chabot had complete control of a supposedly $1,500,000 corporation into which only $14,000 cash had been invested.

Not surprisingly, Anthony was elected president of the corporation. But he then demanded that he also be elected treasurer with full authority to disburse all moneys in the managing of the business according to his own discretion. He would, of course, be responsible to the stockholders at their annual meeting, at which he would have the majority vote. Thus Chabot had absolute and unlimited control of the company.[13]

Anthony then proposed to give Huff and Haslehurst free water for their estates if they would obtain agreements from other landowners on the Creek to allow the California Water Company to divert the Creek. Chabot generously agreed to lay a water main down Ward Avenue (Estudillo), and to allow the inhabitants of San Leandro to subscribe to the service at regular rates. He also gave the people of San Leandro first rights to water from the reservoir as long as the supply lasted. Chabot and Hasslehurst and Huff had planned well. Most landowners had signed even before the first meeting of the company. The remainder signed soon afterwards. Thus by 1874 the new company had water rights below the dam site, for only the cost of free water for two estates. (This cost was not trivial, considering that Haslehurst and Huff had 4,800 and 3,000 square yards of lawn respectively.)[14]

The acquisition of the land for the dam site and the reservoir was more complicated and expensive, but construction of the dam was allowed to begin during the litigation. The California Water Company acquired the right-of-way from the dam site to Oakland at little or no cost. Chabot did have to deed a parcel of land on the hill south of the reservoir to Alameda County, on which he had to build a road to replace the one flooded by the reservoir.[15]

In December 1874, at a rare meeting of the California Water Company stockholders (Anthony could see little need for such meetings), three new stockholders showed up—Henry Pierce, A.J. Pope, and little brother, Remi, all officials of the Contra Costa Water Company. Each new stockholder held one share of stock. Huff and Haslehurst satisfied with their generous deal, resigned as directors and were replaced by Pierce and Pope. No more meetings of the California Water Company were held for a year and a half.[16]

While all these negotiations were taking place, Anthony, with Boardman trailing after him, had started work on the dam in early 1874, with an estimated completion date of summer 1875. Although the work was being done by the California Water Company, it was generally believed by the public and the newspapers that the Contra Costa Water Company was building the new dam. Anthony made no attempt to correct the general impression.

Chabot had also been busy trying to arrange the necessary financing for his project. Anthony's investment of $10,000 in California Water Company stock would get the preliminary work started, but he intended to use borrowed money to build the dam. He always preferred to use other people's money and keep his personal holdings liquid.[17]

But a serious problem arose to plague the Frenchman. In January, 1874, it was proposed in the Oakland City Council that Oakland should own its water works. This was the first of many proposals made during the next few decades for municipalization of the Oakland water supply. In early February the Council submitted a proposed bill to the state legislature which would allow Oakland to take over the water company and its properties.

Surprisingly, Chabot was not upset by the proposal. He might even benefit from it. Anthony indicated that he would not oppose a city buy-out if the price were right, but he also proposed an alternate plan. He suggested that the city lend him credit in city-backed bonds to finish the San Leandro dam. The city would be given the option of purchasing the water system at the end of ten years from the date of the loan. This idea would be highly advantageous to Chabot who was still searching for private capital to build the dam. Public money would be much cheaper. The Oakland power structure approved of Chabot's plan, but a bill to implement it was buried in a legislative committee.

Anthony could not wait on the whims of the legislature. He quickly lined up commitments from private investors, and San Leandro Canyon immediately bustled with activity. Hundreds of Chinese laborers started to dig a ditch across the canyon for the foundation of the puddle wall. Chabot was still convinced that San Leandro water would reach Oakland in 1875.[18]

Then the legislature dropped a bombshell. At the end of March, 1874, it passed a deformed version of the first bill proposed by the city in February. The bill gave Oakland the power to exercise water rights and condemn existing water works, but placed the power to do so in "A Board of Public Works for Oakland." To everyone's fury, the board was to be appointed by the governor, not the City Council. Equally bad, payment for the water works would be in bonds which were not payable in gold. In those days securities not payable in gold sold considerably under face value. Administratively and financially the legislation was weak.

The new law immediately dealt both Chabot and Oakland a serious blow. Anthony's financial backers faded away. San Leandro Canyon fell silent. Dismally, Anthony surveyed the shallow trench, stacks of timbers, scattered pipes, and piles of mud that marked the site of his dream dam.[19]

But a few weeks later, to the relief of the community, the governor appointed five prominent and respected local businessmen to the new Board of Public Works. The fear was dispelled that a group of outside radical politicians might dominate Oakland's water supply. Chabot's backers returned with cash in hand. San Leandro Canyon again bustled with workers. But several precious work weeks had been lost. As a result, Oakland would have a serious water crisis in 1875.[20]

During the next two years, Oakland's city fathers gradually lost interest in municipalization. And, as he watched his new dam grow higher each day, Anthony lost interest in selling. He became very evasive when asked about his terms for selling, and the City Council foresaw a long struggle with the quiet, but stubborn, Frenchman if it tried to take over his company.[21]

At the same time, many civic leaders began to question whether city acquisition of the San Leandro reservoir, or any local water source, would solve the long-range problems of water purity or supply. This attitude was strongly illustrated in January, 1876 (before the San Leandro dam was finished), in a *Tribune* editorial entitled "Nasty Water:"

"If human life were considered of any consequence in this country there would be a law against damming up the canyons and peddling out the accumulated drainings of cow pastures and barnyards... Talk about the deleterious effects of liquor drinking! Why the water furnished to the inhabitants of this city has carried more people to the grave during the past year than all the rot-gut... consumed in this state. At times during the past week the water has been so filthy that a respectable cow would turn away from it in disgust..."

The editorial then went on to condemn the local sources of water, but not Chabot's water company *per se*, and emphasized the need for sources in the Sierra. The rather rabid editorialist was correct. Oakland would not have a satisfactory water supply until 1929, when its pipelines from the East Bay Municipal Utility District's new reservoir in the Sierras poured pure mountain water into the depleted, muddy, local reservoirs. [22]

CHAPTER 11

Oakland Saved

W ith his attentions riveted almost exclusively on his new dam, in 1874 Chabot moved to the Tubbs Hotel in East Oakland, which was further from his office but over a mile closer to the dam. Anthony and his little family, Mary Ann and nine-year-old Ellen (who had been nicknamed Nellie), moved into a spacious suite in the elegant hotel where they lived for over five years.

The Tubbs was Oakland's most luxurious hostelry, and a favorite vacation resort of wealthy Bay Area residents. Surrounded by extensive, beautifully landscaped grounds in which Ellen loved to play, the three-story, turreted structure occupied an

Tubbs Hotel, East Oakland, 1873. Chabot and Mary Ann lived here for about ten years. (Oakland Public Library, Oakland History Room.)

entire block on East 12th Street in East Oakland. An army of chambermaids and valets attended to Mary Ann's every house-keeping need, and the gourmet dining room served the family meals. If she desired to go shopping, she took the horse-car railroad in front of the hotel to Oakland or to the San Francisco ferry. Anthony's horse and buggy were cared for by the stable grooms. The hotel's proprietor, Hiram Tubbs, had been a Bay Area entrepreneur for many years. Hiram and Anthony became close friends. They regularly spent their evenings together in the hotel's comfortable lobby, or in the elegant mahogany bar, dis-cussing their respective businesses and community concerns.[1]

Anthony devoted nearly two years almost exclusively to the San Leandro Dam. He left the day-to-day routine of his Contra Costa Water Company in the hands of Henry Pierce, the vice-president, and brother, Remi, the assistant superintendent. Nearly every day, regardless of weather, from mid-1874 to the summer of 1876 Anthony Chabot rose early. He drove his horse and buggy out the county road (East 14th Street) about ten miles to the San Leandro Dam site. There he personally directed the con-struction of the dam with the assistance of his engineer, William Boardman. As in the case of Temescal, Boardman made the necessary surveys, drawings, and reports, but Anthony imperi-ously made the major decisions based largely on his intuition. Although Chabot's methods of financing the dam may have conflicted with late 20th-century business ethics, there was nothing careless or improper in his construction methods. Nearly 30 years later on April 18, 1906, the great earthquake gave Chabot's dam its supreme test. Five billion gallons of turbulent water were poised to wash San Leandro and thousands of people into San Leandro Bay. But the dam held firm without even a crack. Not bad for an amateur engineer![2]

The construction of the dam presented Anthony with no

formidable engineering difficulties. On the north side of the site a steep hill jutted out into the canyon. Spillways and watermain connections could be tunneled through the hill without having to weaken the dam with those structures. On the south side the banks were almost precipitous. There was plenty of clay for the puddle wall about 300 yards above the site. He had learned from his experience at Temescal; on this dam he first made sure that the bedrock was near the surface before he chose the site. Although the dam was higher than Temescal, it was not quite as long.[3]

In early 1874 Chabot began actual construction. He had started digging the puddle wall when the municipalization crisis temporarily frightened away his backers and closed down the project for many weeks. When work resumed, Chabot still hoped that by the summer of 1875 the dam would be high enough to impound sufficient water to supplement Oakland's supply. Although he wanted to build the dam in record time, Anthony took no shortcuts. Anthony was determined that his finished masterpiece would be indestructible.

While Chabot was digging the foundations for the puddle wall, the usual summer water crisis started in June, 1874. The shortage was not too severe. Chabot lamented that householders let their water flood their lawns all night. The citizens countered that the streets were dusty because the stingy company cut off water for that purpose. But the acrimony was not as bitter as in previous summers, as both sides knew that the dam on San Leandro Creek was actually under way; and each felt certain that there would be no shortages in future years.[4]

Chabot made the puddle wall much stronger than Temescal's. The excavation for the wall's foundation was 90 feet wide and extended from bank to bank, about 300 feet. It was dug down to bedrock, a depth of 10 to 30 feet. Three parallel ditches, three feet deep and three feet wide, were dug the length of the site into the bedrock and filled with concrete to prevent seepage under the dam. Then the entire pit was lined with concrete and filled with thin layers of clay, each of which was wet down and compacted by dozens of horses driven by Chinese laborers. By November the clay puddle wall rose about 20 feet above the surface. Anthony had built a temporary wooden flume to carry San Leandro Creek past the dam until the structure was high enough to hold back the stream.[5]

Then heavy rains pelted the area and the stream began to rise in the flume. As the rains continued, wagons bringing the clay from the sides of the canyon above the dam bogged down in the mud. Horses tamping the puddle wall sank to their bellies. Each day the drenched sixty-one-year-old Frenchman slogged through mud up to his knees shouting orders to add more timbers to the side of the flume. The Chinese laborers worked valiantly, but from every tributary torrential rivulets poured into the rising creek. One day the flume could not handle the runoff. Anthony and his laborers sloshed to higher ground as a lake formed behind the embryonic dam and ate away at the structure. As the dismayed Chabot watched helplessly, the center of the puddle wall gave way. Water poured through the breach carrying 20,000 yards of clay downstream. That evening, before the roaring fire in the Tubbs Hotel lobby, the discouraged Water King poured out his woes to his friend, Hiram. Over half of his puddle wall was washed away. Chabot doubted if his dream dam could be finished by summer 1875.[6]

While repairing the puddle wall, Chabot ordered a tunnel to be run through the hill north of the dam. The mouth of the tunnel was close to the dam near the nose of the hill. This would make a short excavation. This tunnel, only 30 feet above the level of the creek, was designed to connect the reservoir to the watermains leading to Oakland, and also to act as an overflow to reduce the lake level in event of further storms before the dam was built. One

Lake Chabot, under construction, ca. 1875. Note flume on right which sluiced dirt from up the canyon onto the dam. (From John Muir's, "Picturesque California...") [The author is indebted to Jackie Beggs, Lake Chabot dock manager, for sharing this source with him. He also thanks William Sturm, Oakland History Room, for expediting the illustration.]

day Anthony saw Chinese laborers running from the tunnel shrieking in terror. The bore was caving in! The soil close to the nose of the hill was unstable. That evening Hiram heard that a new and longer tunnel would have to be started farther back on the hill. Anthony also confided to his friend that because of this new setback, Oakland would definitely have another long, dry summer in 1875.[7]

Anthony worked feverishly during the winter of 1875. Through the yawning gap in the clay puddle wall, the rain-swollen creek was rushing toward the bay. Chabot heroically tried to fill the breach and raise the dam in time to impound enough of that rainy season's runoff to give Oakland at least a taste of San Leandro water in the coming summer. But it was slow going. Day after day the dispirited Frenchman, knee-deep in mud, watched the clay-filled wagons struggling through the oozy, rutted valley. Frequently the wagons mired down, and extra horses and men struggled to move them. Ever so slowly the breach was filled; layer after layer of clay was thoroughly tamped by exhausted horses. Anthony was determined that the repaired wall would be as strong as before it was breached. He cut no corners. He could take the censure of the thirsty city next summer. But he could not bear even the thought of a disastrous break in his dam. Finally, the 20,000 yards of heavy clay were replaced, and the puddle wall was slowly raised to its planned height.[8]

After the unhappy winter of 1874-75, work on Chabot's dam progressed more rapidly. As the packed, clay puddle wall rose higher, Anthony's spirits also rose. He began supervising the building of ditches and flumes from high up Grass Valley Creek to use water power to sluice dirt and gravel down to the dam site. He enjoyed doing this—it reminded him of his days in Nevada City and Sierra County, and of his flume along the Golden Gate that still carried water to San Francisco. He also ran a high-pressure water system from Grass Valley to which he connected hoses and nozzles at the dam site. These were similar to the water cannon used in hydraulic mining, a process that was then under attack in the courts.

In the spring of 1875, dynamite charges on the hillsides shook the earth as they blasted tons of dirt and gravel into the flumes. This material was carried to the top of the puddle wall and sluiced over the clay. The high-pressure water hoses washed the dirt that had been deposited upon the dam down the front and back of the puddle wall. Temporary levees on the faces of the embankment caught the dirt which was allowed to settle and compact.

Anthony sipped his wine and beamed as he explained sluicing to Hiram. Did Hiram realize that this method of moving dirt, which Anthony had learned in his mining days, cost only one-fourth to one-fifth as much as using horses and wagons? He intended to continue raising the dam by sluicing for many years after its completion, as he had done at Temescal.[9]

While the dam itself was slowly rising during the spring of 1875, Chabot plunged into vital peripheral activities. It was urgent that he start another tunnel to replace the one that had collapsed and connect that tunnel to watermains leading to Oakland.

The new tunnel also was about 30 feet above the creek bed, but was cut through the mountain farther back from the dam. This resulted in a much longer bore than the one that had collapsed. The new tunnel was 860 feet long with about an eight-foot bore. This bore could feed two 24-inch watermains leading to Oakland, or it could allow the water to run off through an open flume into the canyon below the dam. The water flow was controlled from a tower on top of the ridge which was connected by a 157-foot shaft to regulating valves at the mouths of the pipes.[10]

To connect the reservoir to Oakland and to make it possible to get water to the city at the earliest possible moment, Chabot installed a two-foot main from the dam to Fitchberg (present day East 14th Street at 90th Avenue). From this town the watermain followed East 14th Street until it joined the existing Contra Costa Water Company mains in Fruit Vale.[11]

Chabot next started work on a shorter tunnel at a much higher elevation close to the dam. This tunnel also connected with the mains and contained regulating gates to control the lake level.

After his experience with the first tunnel, Anthony took no more chances on cave-ins. He opened a stone quarry about a half-mile upstream and lined both tunnels with masonry. As soon as the water level permitted, he placed a steam launch on the reservoir and hauled the stone to the tunnels in barges.[12]

To replace the old county road that ran up the canyon from San Leandro to Castro Valley, Chabot cut a new road along the side of the hill to the south of the lake. This four-mile stretch of road, somewhat widened and realigned, is still in use today.[13]

When the dam was high enough to begin impounding water, Chabot ordered the clearing of all vegetation from the area to be flooded. This work had to be done by hand. Although the Chinese laborers were low paid, it was still an expensive operation. On this project Anthony did cut corners! He only grubbed 333 acres, far less area than the reservoir would flood; and the work was not done thoroughly. Later the taste of Oakland's water was to betray this negligence. But we can thank Anthony for planting the thousands of trees around the lake that give today's Lake Chabot reservoir and recreation area its park-like appearance.[14]

By early summer the dam rose well above the level of the lower tunnel, and was rising daily as tons of dirt were sluiced over the core. The lower tunnel was complete and connected to the watermains to Oakland. But at the base of the dam, well below the inlet of the lower tunnel, there was only a small pond being fed by the trickling San Leandro Creek.

Despite the slow filling of the reservoir, Oaklanders entered the 1875 dry season as though they had all the water in the world. The demand for water soared. Oakland's population had grown to 25,000, which did not include suburbs like Fruit Vale, and most new residents subscribed to the Contra Costa Water Company. Although the winter rains had filled the Temescal and the Sausal systems, the increased population and the prodigious waste of water soon put a strain on the old system.

In June Chabot asked the city council to allow the water company to shut off the water at night to prevent householders from watering their premises all night long. The city council discreetly sidestepped the issue by replying that this was a matter between a private company and its customers and was not within the jurisdiction of the council. But the proposal brought about a public uproar. The newspapers concentrated on the danger of fire. Chabot backed off. The water stayed on. Chabot did cut off the supply for street sprinkling, and the council discussed the installation of a saltwater sprinkler cart supply tank near the estuary.

The populace noisily complained about the dusty streets, as they soaked their lush, green lawns. But the summer sun dried out the hillsides and the levels of Lake Temescal and the Sausal Reservoir dropped steadily. The water company issued stronger warnings, and most householders reluctantly cut their consumption and grumbled as their lawns turned brown. Anthony anxiously shook his graying head as he told Hiram that this year's drought could bring a serious disaster.[15]

But despite the warm weather, the flow of San Leandro Creek, with its numerous tributaries stretching for miles back into the hills, slowly increased the size of the small lake behind the dam. Finally the muddy water lapped into the lower water tunnel. In mid-September, Anthony quietly filled the mains to Oakland on a trial basis. The Water King had finally brought water, albeit only a trickle, from San Leandro Creek. This proved to be a great mistake!

The exciting news that the mains from San Leandro were filled quickly spread throughout the city. On September 20, 1875, Anthony blanched, but the populace rejoiced, when Oakland's mayor announced to the press that the city now had an unlimited supply of water from the new San Leandro Dam. That evening the city council announced that the saltwater street sprinkling system, which they had not yet started, would not be necessary. Residents rushed to their outside faucets; their sprinklers flooded their parched lawns and dried-up flower beds until the water ran down the gutters.

On the morning of September 23, housewives turned on their faucets to draw water for coffee. Nothing came out! The distributing reservoirs had been drained dry. The water from Temescal and Sausal was absorbed by homes along the mains. Industries which depended upon water, and upon steam engines for power, ground to a halt. The city was completely at the mercy of a fire. The frightened citizens, with barely enough water for drinking purposes, voluntarily conserved water. It was a harrowing few days in Oakland until the distributing reservoirs partially refilled from the meager supplies behind the dams.[16]

The crisis caused another storm of invectives to be loosed against Chabot and his company. But, as in the past, most of the barbs were directed against "the water company," rather than against the mild-mannered little Frenchman who personally seldom stooped to answer his accusers. But the Contra Costa Water Company fiercely countered that the famine was due to citizens who deliberately wasted water. An unnamed company official made a bitter statement to the *Oakland Tribune*:

"Many citizens who would spurn to steal fifty cents steal

water by the hundreds and thousands of gallons; they carelessly and wantonly let the water run at all unseasonable hours, by day and by night, not only irrigating their grounds, but supersaturating them to such an extent that the water flows off the surface and becomes lost, while other citizens are actually suffering for water for household purposes."[17]

The heavy winter rains again quenched the controversy. The flumes sluiced soil over the steadily rising San Leandro Dam as a growing lake formed behind it. On the evening of May 2, 1876, a beaming, triumphant Anthony Chabot raised his glass high and announced to his friend, Hiram, that his dream dam was spilling over. The reservoir then contained at least three billion gallons of water, and would ultimately contain five billion gallons.[18]

May, 1876, was indeed the high point of Anthony's life. His great dam was nearly complete. And now the unassuming Frenchman was ready for the financial killing.

It had been almost three years since Chabot, president of the Contra Costa Water Company, had covertly organized the California Water Company to acquire lands and water rights on San Leandro Creek and to construct the San Leandro Dam.

On May 8, 1876, Anthony Chabot, president of the California Water Company, called to order the first meeting in almost 18 months of its Board of Directors. All of the board members were also affiliated with the Contra Costa Company. The board passed a resolution which authorized Anthony Chabot, personally, to draw as much water as he deemed necessary from San Leandro Reservoir, free of charge, and sell the water to the citizens of San Leandro. With that little coup, Chabot adjourned the meeting.

At its next meeting the board ordered that the entire contingency fund in the company's treasury, a total of $11,154.26, be paid as a dividend. Anthony received two-thirds of the amount, $7,994. He had only contributed $10,000 cash for his stock. Thus, he had built the great dam and spent only $2,000 of his own money. That thought brought a trace of a smile to the Water King's usually grave countenance.[19]

The board next met on May 16, to arrange the final disposition of the California Company. Mr. A. Chabot, president of the California Water Company, with a straight face, announced that he had received from Mr. A. Chabot, president of the Contra Costa Water Company, a copy of a resolution offering to purchase all property and rights of the California Company in consideration of the Contra Costa Company assuming and paying all outstanding debts of the California Water Company.

It was not such a bad deal, but Mr. Chabot of the California Water Company was not going to let Mr. Chabot of the Contra Costa Water Company buy him out that cheaply. In reply, the California Company agreed to the transaction providing that interest be paid at the rate of one percent per month on the assets. The total purchase price was fixed at $806,191.49.

On June 27, Chabot reported that the Contra Costa Water Company had completed the agreement to pay the debts of the California Company, and had paid him the balance of exactly $150,000. The next day, at the last meeting of the California Water Company, the $150,000 was divided among its four stockholders. Chabot stuffed his share, $107,000, in his pocket and solemnly announced that the California Water Company was dissolved.[20]

The California Company died quietly. Anthony carefully laid it to rest. Few people ever knew that it existed, and no newspaper reports mentioned its demise. Its Articles of Incorporation were quietly filed with the county clerk on June 9, 1876, the month of the company's dissolution. The deed that conveyed the company's assets to the Contra Costa Water Company was recorded in the county recorder's office in 1901. The min-

utes of the California Company's board meetings were uncovered by the author in 1948.[21]

Who actually paid the bill for Chabot's dam? The Contra
Costa Water Company stockholders! The company doubled its
capital stock through a sale of a new issue, and thus diluted its
former shareholders' equity and dividends. From this stock sale
about $650,000 was paid to the creditors of the old company in
addition to the $150,000 already paid to the four investors in the
California Company.[22]

Chabot paid part of the price by losing majority interest in his
Contra Costa Water Company. He remained president, and Remi,
as superintendent, supervised the company's facilities; but the
control of the company's community relations came under the
tender mercies of Henry Pierce and his brother, Marshall. When
the company was harshly criticized for its ruthless rate policies
and business practices, Chabot was able to exercise a softening
influence on his ambitious associates. But by 1884, Pierce had
clawed his way to the presidency. The respected Water King was

*Chabot Dam spillway, 1948. Note old hand winches originally used to raise
and lower logs in the slots to control water level.* (Photo by author.)

Chabot Dam, 1948. Headgate of tunnel #2 at right. Low water level was probably due to drought conditions. (Photo by author.)

relegated to a figure-head vice-presidency. Remi retired rather than work under the Pierces. The Chabot dynasty had fallen.[23]

But in the summer of 1876, the citizens of Oakland neither knew nor cared about the financial manipulations and the power struggle inside the water company's doors at 458 Eighth Street. There was plenty of water for the first summer in almost a decade. All traces of animosity toward the water company had disappeared. The three major newspapers now wrote in glowing terms about the new water supply and the Water King who had made it possible. They could not know that Chabot's dam would provide sufficient, if not always pure, water for Oaklanders well into the 20th century.

True, there was an unpleasant, sulphur-like taste to the water, but the Board of Health could find no impurities. Anthony was embarrassed when the board suggested that the taste was due to decaying vegetable matter. Someone had slipped up on the grubbing and left a small orchard beneath the surface. But the city was assured that the water was safe, and the slight taste and odor would soon disappear.[24]

The Board of Health was correct. The objectionable odor and taste disappeared—or possibly people became used to it. On November 2, 1876, a most unusual item appeared in the usually critical *Tribune*:

"There are no more complaints about the city water. The late rains have purified the reservoir's contents and ye Oaklander rejoiceth."

CHAPTER 12

Capitalist & Gentleman Farmer

A "new" Anthony emerged after the completion of San Leandro Dam. During the last eleven years of his life, the controversial "Water King" became the respected and revered "grand old man" of Oakland.

Despite his gradual loss of complete control over the Contra Costa Water Company, he kept his office at 458 Eighth Street for the rest of his life. But he cast off his muddy boots and rain gear and gave his title of superintendent to Remi. The aging Anthony was now content to sit behind his desk as president and, after 1884, as vice-president. There were no more big dam projects, or serious water crises, to occupy his time. The "Water King's" construction days were at an end.[1]

But Chabot's presence in the office cast a moderating influence on Marshall Pierce's policies concerning water rates. Marshall, who had charge of the office, would have liked more autonomy. He complained in letters to his son that he was overworked handling the constant complaints about the high water rates. He had had no vacation in two years. "No let up, only…to do my master's will, A Chabot. Not a bad man but it's daily service under the eye of a master."

However, Marshall's master always had a soft spot for young people. After Marshall's daughter, Nan, had wheedled from Chabot free space at the company's stables for a borrowed horse, she wrote to her brother, "…both of the Chabots are great friends of mine and while they are cross to some people they are *very* kind to me."[2]

But Anthony's boundless energies quickly overflowed his routine duties in the Contra Costa Water Company. His active mind soon plunged him into a wide variety of activities ranging from iron works to paper pulp, from wheat to Japanese tea plants, from astronomy to cranberries. His capital helped develop some of the West Coast's leading industries.

Chabot recalled the days of his youth when he had only pennies to jingle in his pocket, and he now resolved to give away some of his million-dollar fortune to worthy charities and civic institutions. Second only to his water activities, Chabot is known for his philanthropy.

Although his prominent friends and acquaintances urged him to enter politics, Anthony wisely declined that honor. He no longer wished to struggle against the tides of fickle public opinion. He did join the Society of California Pioneers and became an officer of that group of pre-1850 California settlers. He also joined the Live Oak Masonic Lodge in Oakland and attained the honor of 33rd degree Scottish Rite. But despite these exceptions, the quiet, bespeckled, white-haired, little Frenchman was not a "joiner."[3]

Mary Ann, who had left a comfortable home in Lynn, probably told the semi-retired "grand old man" that his family should have a gracious home like other prominent Oaklanders. Remi's family lived in a comfortable home—why not Anthony's family? Anthony had seen the palatial homes of his role models crowning Nob Hill in San Francisco, as well as the attractive homes of his acquaintances in Oakland and its suburbs. But he had been too busy, and a home seems to have been low on Anthony's priorities. He remained at the Tubbs Hotel until 1880, when he finally moved to a house on Fourth Avenue about three blocks from the hotel.[4]

The following year he moved into a spacious East Oakland

Anthony Chabot Residence, built 1882, 104 E. 15th Street, overlooking Lake Merritt. Chabot lived there only five years before his death. Mary Ann died there in 1904. (Oakland Public Library, Oakland History Room.)

home on a slope overlooking Lake Merritt at 104 E.15th Street. Visitors were impressed with the two-story entrance hall with a second story balustrade. From the bay windows of the parlor and second story bedroom, there was a sweeping view of Oakland with its lake in the foreground. A third story tower rising from the middle of the house provided a panoramic view from the Oakland hills across the bay to San Francisco and the Golden Gate. These views were especially stunning at sunset. The lot was deep enough for a barn with two cows and Anthony's horse and buggy. Chabot only lived in his home for about five years before his death. The house was torn down in 1951.[5]

After ten years of being cooped-up in a hotel, this roomy home, with the finest furnishings money could buy, was the highlight of Mary Ann's married life. She seldom left her stately dwelling during the next twenty-two years of her life. Apparently well-educated, she loved books, and read extensively. But she entertained very seldom and hated to travel. On a rare trip to the East Coast, she sat up most of the way.[6]

Mary Ann's life revolved around her beloved step-daughter, Ellen, popularly nicknamed Nellie during her early life. Ellen grew into a spindly, wiry, gray-eyed towhead. She had a quick mind and was likely educated in local private schools. She was enrolled in a New York college when she was 22, but her father's final illness soon brought her back to Oakland.

Anthony could not have had much time for Ellen during her childhood, but he loved her dearly. As she matured into an active, inquisitive young lady, he began to lay plans to have her join his business and philanthropic activities. He showed his trust in her judgment by appointing her a trustee of his last great charity, a women's sheltering home. He also named her as an executor of his estate.[7]

But Anthony spent little time enjoying the comfort of his home and his little family. His days were filled with business and philanthropic activities. And nearly every evening he left Mary Ann alone with Ellen and strode four blocks to the Tubbs Hotel. Here he joined his old friend, Hiram, who no longer owned the hotel, but also lived nearby. They sometimes met with other leading citizens of the community, and business and philanthropic plans were hatched. Frequently the two friends just sat and talked late into the evening.[8]

Only one person was closer to Anthony than Hiram. That was his brother Remi. From that day in 1850 when he joined Anthony at Nevada City, Remi was associated in almost all of Anthony's projects. Only during Anthony's eastern odyssey, in the early 1860's, were the two brothers separated. As superintendent of the Contra Costa Water Company, Remi relieved his brother of the details of running the company, allowing Anthony more time for other business and philanthropic ventures. But in 1884, with Henry Pierce actively running the company as president, Remi resigned from the water business. He became a self-styled "Capitalist," as did many men of wealth in that golden age when "Capitalist" was not a dirty name.[9]

The tall, distinguished-looking Remi was not an *habitué* of the Tubbs Hotel lounge. Remi was devoted to his beautiful Emelie and their lovely daughters. Altogether, Remi and Emelie had five children. After Henrietta, they had a boy, Joseph Anthony, named after Remi's father and brother. But the boy died only a few weeks after his birth in 1873. The family patriarch's name and the name of Anthony's beloved were perpetuated through the next child—Josephine Ellen—born two year's later. Daughters Catherine and Clara followed during the next six years.[10]

In a brotherly way, Anthony was attracted to the beautiful and energetic Emelie. He had never known a woman like her. Although she was a loving wife and mother, Emelie was not the typical 19th century housewife. She had a classical education, was an accomplished musician, and made the most of her gifted mind. Like her brother-in-law, she was restless and ever turning to new ventures. But unlike Anthony, she was outgoing and not lost in a crowd.

Anthony also loved his four nieces who, in turn, adored their Uncle Anthony. On many an afternoon the children shrieked with delight as their uncle's carriage stopped in front of their house. With a smile on his lined face, he would bring them boxes of fruit and other gifts. He would then visit with Emelie and discuss their favorite subject, charities.

Where charity was concerned, Emelie Chabot was a household word. She was an organizer, had business ability, and was not afraid of hard work. For example, she organized charity entertainments at the San Francisco Opera House; she headed the Ladies' Relief Society; and she was a founding member and lifetime officer of the Fabiola Hospital Association, Oakland's first major hospital. In one of those afternoon conversations, Emelie sweetly talked her brother-in-law into contributing the original plot of land, worth nearly $3,000, for the hospital. Part of Kaiser Hospital occupies the site today.

Unlike Anthony, Emelie was a devout Catholic and devoted considerable time to activities at St. Francis de Sales Church. She was also a member of early-day women's rights groups and attended meetings sponsored by Susan B. Anthony. In today's parlance, Emelie would be called a feminist. Unlike her reclusive sister-in-law, Emelie traveled widely. She liked to travel so well that she gave one of her daughters a European trip as a wedding present, and then joined the bride and groom on their honeymoon![11]

Anthony respected Emelie's business acumen and organizing ability. In the early 1870's he appointed her secretary of the Contra Costa Water Company. This position was short-lived due to her second pregnancy. But a decade later, as we shall see, Emelie was made corporate secretary for Anthony's extensive cranberry venture. Along with his daughter, Ellen, Anthony included Emelie as a trustee in his women's sheltering home. It is noteworthy that there is no record of Chabot appointing Mary Ann to any position.

Despite her many activities, Remi's wife was the family hostess. At least three Chabot relatives, brother Toussaint, and nephews John and Robert, visited California and stayed at Remi's home. Robert, of whom we will speak later, remained for many months. Toussaint visited Remi on two occasions, and was present during his final illness. There is no record of family visits to the Anthony Chabot home.[12]

From his desk at the water company, or in the lounge at the Tubbs Hotel, the Water King planned ways to invest his vast fortune. He still owned a substantial share of the Contra Costa Water Company; and, although he had lost interest in the San Jose Water Company, he retained his financial and management interest in the Vallejo City Water Works. But this was not enough to satisfy Chabot's still restless spirit. He needed new outlets for his growing fortune.

Anthony soon had investments, large and small, in over a score of companies. His financial assistance brought success to many businesses in Chabot's adopted city. The *Oakland Daily Evening Tribune* reported: "He [Chabot] was always busy, and was no coward in making investments which would benefit a community even though he knew his returns would be small." On the other hand, the more cynical *Morning Times* stated: "Mr. Chabot was tireless in his investments and took hold of everything that came along in which he saw money." Probably both views are correct. There is no doubt that Anthony, from the days of his youth, always had the touch of Midas.[13]

Chabot's investments helped start two major Oakland area companies. In 1885 Chabot heavily backed the formation of the California Cotton Mills of East Oakland, capitalized at over a half million dollars. This business not only benefited Oakland but promoted the cotton industry in California. The company flourished until the 1950's when the mill closed. Its brick building, long an East Oakland landmark, may still be seen near the foot of 23rd Avenue.

When his friend, Egbert Judson, needed a little cash to start the Judson Manufacturing Company of Emeryville (still in business today as the Judson Steel Company), Chabot handed him $55,000, secured by bonds, notes, and common stock. The Judson company at that time manufactured agricultural implements and other iron and steel products. For many years Chabot was a major stockholder and an officer of the corporation.[14]

Anthony's investments were not confined to Oakland. In 1885, Chabot and Judson joined the Towle brothers in the incorporation of the Pioneer Pulp Company in Placer county. Located at the headquarters of the Towle Brothers' lumber business, the company manufactured a variety of paper and paper pulp products. Chabot also bought an interest in the California Paper Company in Stockton which was headed by his associate, Henry Pierce.

Aside from the Contra Costa Water Company, the Water King's largest investment was in the Puget Sound Iron Company, a California corporation. Chabot sunk close to $100,000 in this company. It had an iron and steel manufacturing works at Port Townsend, and also engaged in iron ore mining nearby.[15]

Anthony never really gave up his fascination with mining. He and Remi had rich gold gravel claims in Placer and Calaveras counties; both mines yielded the brothers handsome returns. From time to time he invested in mines in other western states.

Anthony's "Midas' Touch" also brought him gold from Oakland's real estate. He perceived that the business district was expanding east of Broadway. So he purchased residential property in the path of the commercial expansion. East Oakland's gently rolling foothills, known as Highland Park (near present Highland Hospital), were being laid out by developers for residential use. Anthony bought a number of plots which quickly soared in value.[16]

One might think that Chabot, who had run away from the family farm in Quebec, would have nothing to do with agriculture or horticulture. But he took an intense interest in both fields, especially the latter, although it is doubtful that he personally ever dug in the soil.

In the agricultural field, Anthony had a profitable 1,200-acre ranch in the Livermore Valley about four miles from Pleasanton. Again he picked the right place and time for his venture. The valley was booming. Crops and passengers could now be carried from the valley to Oakland by the Central Pacific Railroad in a few pleasant hours via scenic Niles Canyon. Previously the journey was over a slow, tortuous, steep wagon road through hills west of Dublin. Anthony frequently was seen riding from the Pleasanton station past the neat, white homes of the growing community on the way to his ranch. His grain and cereal crops brought a good price in the Oakland market.[17]

On the east shore of Lake Temescal, Chabot owned 160 acres of land which had originally been acquired by the water company. The acreage was later sold by the water company to President Chabot for the reasonable sum of one dollar. The caretaker of the reservoir lived on this land. His house remained until it burned during World War II. Anthony also used the land for a profitable 50-acre fruit orchard.

But the Temescal tract was better known throughout the Oakland area for Anthony's Oriental gardens which he planted and maintained at considerable expense. It is said that he entertained a Japanese prince for a few days at his home, and the prince, in return, sent him rare Oriental trees and plants. In his

Temescal gardens he grew tea plants and other exotic Oriental trees. According to the *Oakland Enquirer*, the tea cured in these gardens was said by "the nobility of China who have visited this coast" to be equal to the teas of China. Remi's daughters, at a much later date, remembered the tea as too bitter. Nevertheless, Anthony was proud to have proved that Oriental tea could be grown in this climate.

Chabot had a second nursery of rare plants, many Oriental, on a lot near his home. Here he employed a Japanese, named Domato, to maintain this Oakland show place. It is said that some of the first camelias, persimmons, flowering quince, and Japanese magnolias ever to bloom in California were in Anthony Chabot's East Oakland garden.[18]

Anthony's outstanding agricultural achievement was the first successful commercial cranberry cultivation on the Pacific Coast. Visitors from the Bay Area are surprised to find on the Long Beach Peninsula resort area of Washington the site of the Anthony Chabot Cranberry Bog.

About 1870, Anthony's brother-in-law from Massachusetts visited the Long Beach Peninsula on the south coast of Washington. Here he was surprised to find marshy, acid, peat soil which reminded him of the cranberry bogs on Cape Cod. He may have learned that the local Indians had used small, bitter, wild cranberries for food. There are reports that the Washington Indians near the mouth of the Columbia had supplied the Lewis and Clark expedition, as well as several early voyagers, with the fruit.

Despite the fact that there had been one or two recent unsuccessful attempts at cranberry cultivation on the Long Beach Peninsula, Chabot's brother-in-law thought the area had the potential to be another Cape Cod. Not only did the area have the right soil and weather conditions for the low-growing, trailing vines, but there was a good supply of water. This was necessary for irrigation and the protection of the tender berries from both frost and excessive heat. His face lighted up. He could import choice vines from Cape Cod, cultivate them properly, and make a fortune.

There was only one hitch. He did not have the capital. But he knew someone who did have the capital, and who was always looking for a profitable investment.[19]

Although he was busy with three water companies, the Water King listened attentively to his brother-in-law's plans. His relative proposed to move to Washington, bring the appropriate Cape Cod plants with him, and plant and tend the bog. Anthony, and possibly others, would supply the money. Government lands in the Territory (Washington was not yet a state) could be had for almost nothing. And his brother-in-law had conveniently brought a list of some of the best available tracts for cranberry cultivation. After working out the financial details, the relatives shook hands. It was a deal!

Between 1872 and 1877 Anthony obtained patents for nearly 1,600 acres of government land on the Long Beach Peninsula. As he had other commitments, much of this land was purchased in conjunction with Henry Pierce, and two other associates, A.J. Pope and W.C. Talbot.[20]

Meanwhile, his brother-in-law returned home to pack up his belongings and his family, and to gather some choice cranberry plants. He expansively described his plans. Soon his family would be living in Ilwaco on the coast of Washington. Then the plan abruptly exploded! Anthony's French Canadian sister made it clear to her husband that she was not leaving her comfortable Massachusetts' home for any "Ilwaco."

Probably the brother-in-law still worked on the project. He likely procured the proper vines for the bog, and may also have found a Netherlander from New Jersey who knew cranberry culture. This unnamed Dutchman came west to plant the bog in lieu of Chabot's frustrated relative.[21]

Anthony, who knew nothing about cranberries, had to depend upon his new Dutch associate to develop his bog. About 1880 the Netherlander selected 35 ideal acres. First he leveled the land. Next he "scalped" off a thin layer of the ground over which he spread a layer of peat moss topped with a fine layer of sand. He then planted six-inch cuttings of McFarland cranberry vines imported from Cape Cod. They immediately took root. All Anthony had to do was to wait patiently for about three years for the harvest.[22]

But the Water King was not a patient man, and he was worried about being personally liable for a far-away venture about which he knew so little and had so little control. Also Chabot was not happy with his foreman. It is likely that the distance and a language barrier made communications with the Netherlander difficult. Anthony decided to form a corporation to cloak his personal liability and to provide a more efficient organization.

In the spring of 1883 Anthony gathered with some old cronies, and discussed the incorporation of a cranberry company. The group included his brother, his old friends Hiram Tubbs and Frank Shattuck, and an acquaintance, George Grant. George, an 1850 pioneer, was a well-known East Oakland wholesale grocer with stores in other towns. Obviously, George could provide marketing expertise and a local market for cranberries.

The five men incorporated the Pacific Cranberry Company on June 2, 1883, with its main office in Oakland. Although its authorized capitalization was $100,000, the organizers only invested $500 each. Anthony was elected president of the company, and he appointed Remi's wife, Emelie, as secretary. Anthony and Henry Pierce then sold for $1,000 the Washington land patents

Anthony Chabot established the first commercial cranberry bog in south-west Washington. His descendants, Elwell, Jim, and Jeff Chabot still grow cranberries in the area. (The Sou'wester, "Pacific County [Wash.] Historical Society," Autumn 1983.)

they jointly owned (they had earlier bought out the other two men) to the Pacific Cranberry Company. In September Anthony and Emelie increased the company's liquidity by selling land not needed for cranberries on the peninsula.[23]

Meanwhile, the Chabots selected a new agent to live in Ilwaco with full power to operate the cranberry bog for the Pacific Cranberry Company. Back in the late 1870's, Robert Chabot, a nephew from Canada, an ambitious young man of 17, had arrived in Oakland. Anthony gave him a job in the water company's pipe yard under Remi. Remi and Emelie took Robert into their home; he may have been a surrogate for their only son who had died. Now 22, the young man was asked by his uncles to join in the cranberry venture as their agent on the Long Beach Peninsula.

Time was running out. The first crop of berries would be ready for harvesting in the fall of 1883, and Robert knew little more about cranberries than did his uncles. He hastened to Ilwaco where he quickly fired the Netherlander. He then hired an assistant, Bion A. Landers from the Massachusetts bog country, who was experienced in cranberry culture.

The first crop was a success, and for many years the bog made money. Robert and Bion worked well together, and Robert quickly learned the cranberry business. He lived in Ilwaco, married a young teacher, and started a family. His uncles, satisfied with their profits, visited the bog only on rare occasions. They should have stayed home. Remi went north in late 1884, and fractured a leg while passing through Astoria. Anthony went up three years later, where he caught a severe cold that contributed to his final illness.[24]

In 1892, Robert, now experienced in cranberry culture, grew restless. Both Anthony and Remi had died. Emelie owned a controlling interest in the cranberry company, but may have lost her enthusiasm for the venture. Robert resigned and moved farther up the Washington coast to start his own cranberry bog. Landers quit soon afterwards.

By 1904 the bog had gone to weeds and was sold. But the Chabot name returned to the area in 1947 when Elwell Chabot, Robert's youngest son, came to the peninsula and started a bog near the old Chabot property. His son, James, now operates the business. And the original Chabot bog is again producing cranberries under a new owner.[25]

CHAPTER 13

Philanthropist

The evenings at the Tubbs Hotel resulted not only in many profitable business deals for Chabot, but also in many benefits for Oakland and nearby communities. During the latter part of his life, Chabot became better known for his philanthropies than for any of his other activities. In fact, he was one of the most generous individual philanthropists in the history of the East Bay. Many of his ideas for civic projects came from his conversations at the Tubbs with Hiram and other cronies.

His philanthropic instincts likely stem from two different sources. Anthony knew real poverty after he ran away from home, and also must have observed the human degradation in the New York slums where people were worse off than he. Now he was in a financial position to help unfortunate people. Also some of his shrewd business transactions, such as the California Water Company, while not illegal at that time, could have weighed a bit upon his conscience. Giving back a substantial portion of those gains to the community would be a subconscious form of penance. One thing is certain, he enjoyed no tax write-offs for his contributions. There was no income tax.

At any rate, the Water King's charities of his later years, as well as the abundant water from his San Leandro reservoir, erased most of the public's negativism toward the benign little Frenchman. Even the high rates and arrogance of the water company were blamed on Henry Pierce and his appointees, but not on Anthony.

It will never be known how much Chabot gave to charities

and civic projects. While his large gifts, in one case over
$100,000, could not be kept secret, no one knows how much he
gave to individuals and small charities. He was very
uncommunicative about his individual charity contributions and
did not even inform Hiram. Anthony drew his own checks. No
one but his silent banker knew the amounts he wrote for miscellaneous donations. His obituary in the *Tribune* states that:
"Modestly and quietly he went about his well-doing, never her-
alding his deeds abroad." His daughter stated that his wallet was
always open to the poor and the needy. Although his donations
were usually to local people and organizations, he did send $100
to a charity in Iceland.[1]

Anthony's charities extended to his own family when they
were in need. He loaned $7,500 to Edward Chabot, which was
never repaid. As the Chabot family was very large, it is likely that
he assisted others of his kin. His charity also extended to the
family of his first wife. He loaned $2,100 to Samuel Hasty and
forgave the debt in his will. Nepotism did not bother Anthony. In
addition to Remi, he gave jobs to his brother, John, and his
nephew, Robert.

Although Anthony belonged to no church, he donated gener-
ously to religious causes. He gave $500 to the building fund for
St. Anthony's Catholic Church in East Oakland. But to prove his
ecumenism, he also generously aided the building funds at the
Hebrew Congregation, and the Swedish Methodist and
Baptist churches. He then gave several pews to the First
Congregational Church.[2]

Whenever a charitable subscription was being circulated, the
fund raisers always sought out Anthony. They knew they could
find him most evenings at Tubbs. Anthony would usually be the
first to subscribe, and would donate the largest amount.

One night a group of war veterans, including Hiram, was

meeting at the hotel. They had been trying to raise $3,000 to build a cottage, to be called the Oakland Cottage, at the new Veterans' Home near Yountsville in Napa County. They had circulated subscriptions among local veterans without much success. Then in walked Anthony, a non-veteran. He quietly reached into his pocket and with no fanfare drew out a thousand dollars. This got the enterprise rolling, and the balance was soon raised. Chabot also furnished the cottage, provided it with drains and a sewer, and donated a horse and cart. Although he did not wish it, the building was named the Chabot Cottage.[3]

With Anthony's abounding generosity, it was easy for Emelie, as we mentioned in the previous chapter, to talk her brother-in-law into donating to her favorite charity, the Fabiola Hospital Association. In the summer of 1887, a few months before his death, the ladies of the association had decided on the corner of Moss Avenue (MacArthur) and Broadway for the location of their hospital. At Emelie's urging, Anthony visited the site, and was pleased with the location. He found that a bank owned the land. After a bit of haggling, Chabot got the property for $2,800 and deeded it to the association. This humanitarian memorial to Oakland's benefactor was completed about a year after Anthony's death.[4]

Emelie easily talked Anthony into contributing heavily to another of her expensive charities—The Ladies' Relief Society. He largely financed the construction of the Old Ladies' Home, which was operated by the society. Also, from time to time he contributed a thousand dollars for its maintenance and operation. It is estimated that his gifts to this home amounted to $25,000. In addition, he often donated food to the institution. One of his donations showed that he did have a wry sense of humor. Anthony purchased a flock of turkeys, had them taken to the home, and released into the yard. He watched in amusement as

Home for Aged Women, Oakland. Largely financed and supported by Chabot. (Oakland Public Library, Oakland History Room).

startled, gray heads kept popping out of the windows to investigate the ensuing cacophonous gobbling and flapping of wings.[5]

Anthony was concerned as he walked down Broadway, and women of apparent respectability and good character would beg him for money. He was always a "soft touch," and gave generously to the supplicants. He found that many of these homeless, impoverished women had led respectable, normal lives, and that many had small children. Most had been reduced to begging after being widowed or deserted by their husbands. They were looking for work, but the compassionate, gray-bearded Frenchman knew that many would be driven to the miserable poorhouse or into crime or vice as a means of survival.

Emelie's Ladies' Relief Society Home could not help. It provided permanent shelter for destitute older women who could no longer work. Anthony envisioned a temporary home for impoverished women who were looking for work and wanted to rehabilitate themselves.

In July, 1887, Anthony organized the Women's Sheltering and Protection Home of Oakland. The stated purpose of this home was to provide temporary housing for women of good moral character who were widows, or had been deserted by their husbands, and who were seeking work. It also provided shelter for the children of these women—the first "day care center"— until their mothers could again provide them with a home.

A board of trustees was established to administer the home and its property. The board was to consist of five men and four women. (This "affirmative action" concept may well be the result of Emelie's influence on her brother-in-law.) Ellen Chabot, then 22, and Emelie were among the board members.

This home was a "big ticket" item—Anthony's most expensive donation. Chabot donated a parcel of land at 9th and Franklin streets in Oakland, and $25,000 in cash for the erection of a

Women's Sheltering & Protection Home of Oakland. Chabot's most generous gift to Oakland (over $100,000). This institution continued well into the present century. (Oakland Public Library, Oakland History Room.)

building. He also gave the institution the stock he owned in several East Bay enterprises and $20,000 in the bonds of the Judson Manufacturing Company. Altogether Chabot donated over $100,000 for this sheltering home which, completed after his death, remained an Oakland institution well into the present century.[6]

One day Anthony was approached by a man who suggested a plan for a home for destitute old men. Anthony's usually calm demeanor bristled. His social philosophy was summed up in his answer:

No, a home for old men is not needed. It would do more harm than good. There is the best reason why many deserving old ladies should be provided for, there is no good reason why any large number of old men should be destitute. If they are it is good proof that they have been intemperate or improvident and to provide a home for such would be but encouragement for such life.[7]

The best-known and most widely used present-day monument to Chabot's philanthropy is the Chabot Observatory and Science Center in the Oakland hills. This unique, publicly owned, astronomical observatory had its origins in the early 1880's.

J.C. Gilson, an astronomy enthusiast, was elected Superintendent of Schools in 1882. He came into the position with a cherished dream—a fully equipped, city owned, astronomical observatory operated and maintained for public use by the Board of Education. His contagious enthusiasm spread to the school board members, especially W. H. Jordan, who decided to raise the necessary funds for the project by public subscription. It was felt that if they could first persuade someone to buy a telescope, the money for the building could be raised by entertainments and other events.

Naturally, Anthony Chabot was the first person they thought of. Gilson just happened to meet Anthony one day and began to discuss astronomy. The subject sparked the Water King's interest. Gilson also just happened to have two astronomy books with him, favorites at the time, one by Proctor and the other by Newcomb. Anthony browsed the books with obvious interest, and asked if he could borrow them. The subject matter appealed to Anthony's keen mind, and he became an astronomy buff for the rest of his life. Gilson then contacted Alvan Clark and Son, a leading telescope maker, and found that an 8-inch refracting telescope would cost $3,000. The rest was easy. Mr. Jordan met with Anthony and discussed the plan for an observatory. Anthony put $3,000 in a special account and told Jordan to order the telescope.[8]

Next came the matter of raising subscriptions for the observatory building. Gilson and Jordan invited the leading men of the community to an astronomy lecture at which the plan was outlined, and subscriptions for a $2,000 building were requested. The fund-raiser fell flat. Only $125 was subscribed! Many in the audience said that Chabot had already given so much that he would get all the glory, and that they were loath to give under those circumstances.

The next day Anthony looked up from his office desk. There stood Gilson and Jordan rather red-faced and embarrassed. They explained that the telescope had been ordered, but there was no place to house it. Anthony smiled knowingly, took out his checkbook and asked the price. The two educators looked at each other, and Gilson suggested $2,000.[9]

The City Council locked Chabot into the deal. On April 16, 1883, the council passed an ordinance which granted A. Chabot the right and permission to construct, at his own expense, an astronomical observatory, equipped with an equatorially mounted eight-inch telescope, on Lafayette Square (a public park bounded by Jefferson, Grove, 10th, and 11th streets). He was to construct the observatory according to specifications approved by the Board of Education. Chabot was then to vest full title to the observatory in the Board of Education, to be held in trust for the city of Oakland. It was further provided that the observatory and the telescope should be used without charge or expense by both the public schools and the general public under rules to be prescribed by the Board of Education.[10]

The foundation stone was laid on May 22 with an elaborate ceremony attended by many dignitaries including, of course, the mayor and leading school board members. The civic leaders were all milling around on the platform trying to outtalk each other, as the shy little Frenchman, who had made the occasion possible, arrived. Anthony disliked such pomposity, and, after a few pleasantries, quietly took his seat. The *Times* reported that of all those present, Chabot was the "most modest and retiring of any."

The square was packed with enthusiastic citizens and also with hundreds of noisy schoolchildren who were happy to have the afternoon away from classes. A male quartet, which was scheduled to begin the ceremony with a song, hovered near the platform. The honored guests took their seats. The crowd quieted. Mayor Martin signed the quartet to come forward.

The quartet approached the platform. The group was led by Mr. Share, a distinguished looking gentleman of regal bearing. The schoolchildren edged forward with suppressed giggles and conspiratorial grins. Mr. Share stepped upon the platform, bowed to the mayor and guests. As Share turned toward his audience, the citizenry cheered and applauded. The children screamed wildly and rushed forward showering the bewildered baritone with flowers. Share was virtually buried beneath an avalanche of fragrant blossoms which covered the stand. Anthony looked on with an amused smile, realizing that he was supposed to have been the target of the floral bombardment.

The crowd finally quieted. The nonplused quartet sang the "Lord's Prayer." The jubilant children, unaware of their mistake, sang "Our Native Land." Mayor Martin, Mr. Gilson, and others made long speeches with occasional references to Mr. Chabot's generosity and contribution to science. With much ceremony, and more oratory, the foundation stone was laid along with documents pertaining to the observatory. Anthony Chabot sat quietly. He was not called upon to speak. Finally, Reverend McLean, of the Congregational Church, intoned a prayer. The quartet then led the audience in "America."

The crowd was about ready to disperse. There were frantic whisperings between the dignitaries. They had forgotten to introduce the guest of honor! Mr. Jordan shouted for the crowd's attention. He called Chabot to the front, introduced him to the audience, and explained how the children had honored the wrong man. The crowd cheered lustily. A few left-over bouquets were handed to the observatory's benefactor. The embarrassed little Frenchman bowed politely, but made no speech. After the usual handshakes he walked briskly away, chuckling to himself over the fiasco.[11]

The building was no sooner started than Gilson and Jordan, with hats in hand, again approached Chabot. They explained that after examining the plans, the Board of Education felt that the $2,000 building would be quite shabby for a $3,000 telescope. The building would not be a credit to the community. Anthony agreed that it should be an appropriate building. How much? The supplicants hesitatingly replied that it would be around eight or nine thousand. To their relief, the mild little man nodded his assent. In November that year the building was finished and the telescope installed. The building was dedicated and named, at Chabot's request, "Oakland Observatory." But that name did not stick! Over the Frenchman's objections, it was always known as "Chabot Observatory."[12]

After the dedication Chabot was again called upon. Astronomers were complaining that the telescope alone could not be used for serious astronomical research. So Anthony again displayed his patience and liberality by paying for a four-inch transit, a mean-time clock, a sidereal clock, and a spectroscope. These, plus a few other little items, brought the total tab to over $15,000.[13]

The observatory was an immediate success. But the building soon proved inadequate. It had been poorly designed, with a tall tower shaped like a water tank which housed the telescope. The telescope could be reached only by a narrow, crooked staircase

The original Chabot Observatory, mid-1880s, financed by Anthony Chabot. Its eight-inch telescope is still in use in the Chabot Observatory and Science Center in the East Oakland Hills. (Oakland Public Library, Oakland History Room.)

that entered the observing room through a trap door. The "mucilage bottle," as the structure was popularly called, could scarcely accommodate the long lines of eager visitors.

Anthony was pleased with his creation and its overwhelming public acceptance. He offered to enlarge the building. Professional astronomers helped the school board draw up plans for a larger building with a 12-inch telescope. In the fall of 1887, Chabot was to meet with the committee to approve the plans and the costs. But he missed a train from his ranch in the Livermore Valley and could not attend. Before a new meeting could be arranged he was taken ill, and the plans for a 12-inch telescope died with him. But Chabot would have been delighted to know that shortly after his death, the observatory's director, Charles Burckhalter, discovered a comet with the eight-inch telescope.[14]

However, in his will Chabot took care of the future of his beloved observatory, by providing a $10,000 endowment to be

Remodeled Chabot Observatory, 1892. This building eliminated the winding staircase to the telescope that plagued the staff of the first building. (Oakland Public Library, Oakland History Room.)

beloved observatory, by providing a $10,000 endowment to be used to increase the size of the institution. The interest on this amount was used in 1892 to erect a new building "with a civilized way of reaching the telescope." But the new building also had a defect. The chimney from the stove in the waiting room blew its smoke directly into the telescope's dome. So when the telescope was in use, the waiting room was cold. This building, called Chabot Hall, remained in Lafayette Square until the late 1920's, but at the time of its construction bright electric lights were replacing the soft glow of gas lights in the growing city. The urban glare soon spoiled the astronomers' vista of the heavens.[15]

A new location was sought for the observatory up in the Oakland hills away from the city's lights. Mills College donated a site back of the college. In 1916 a new observatory with a 20-inch telescope, in addition to the original eight-inch instrument, was completed. The cost of the new telescope and building was substantially defrayed by Anthony Chabot's endowment.[16]

In recent years the use of Chabot Observatory's telescopes has again been impaired by the glare of the sprawling city, and a new site is being considered. But this lasting memorial to Anthony Chabot's generosity is still visited by over 30,000 people each year.[17]

CHAPTER 14

Oakland Mourns

L ike many self-made men with little formal education, Anthony wanted his only child to have a college degree. In June, 1887, he accompanied Ellen and Mary Ann to New York where he enrolled Ellen in an exclusive college. Despite the press of his many business and philanthropic activities, Anthony amazed and concerned his friends by remaining in the East for nearly two months.

Although he seldom admitted it, the Water King had not felt well for over three years. A liver ailment was gradually getting worse. In fact, he made his will just before going on the trip. Anthony may have suspected that this could be his last visit to the East; so he made a leisurely tour of Quebec and Maine. He visited his favorite sister, Modiste, in Montreal and discussed his will with her. Other family members were in nearby St. Hyacinthe. At Standish, Maine, Antoine was once again near to his dear Ellen, and his eyes focused on the last few words on her monument "...we hope to meet thee among the blest."

When Chabot arrived in Lynn where Mary Ann was enjoying a visit with her many friends and relatives, his wife coldly told him that she was not returning to Oakland for a while. His activities left her alone most of the time, and with Ellen away, Mary Ann could look forward to an even more lonely life.[1]

In September he made a ten-day inspection tour of his properties in Washington Territory—his cranberry bog near Long Beach and the iron works near Port Townsend. He returned from the North with a serious cold, and he was tenderly pampered at

Remi's home by Emelie and her girls.[2]

But Anthony would not be kept down. He realized that time was short, and returned too soon to his busy work schedule. In mid-October his cold grew worse from exposure. At the same time his liver became inflamed, and he also developed fluids in his lungs. Again Emelie lovingly nursed him at their home at 11th and Madison streets, while Mary Ann remained in Lynn. Dr. J.S. Adams was called, and he and a consulting doctor removed the fluids from Anthony's lungs.

The patient rallied, and, despite Emelie's pleading and the doctor's warnings, Anthony again became a whirlwind of activity. He traveled to the Livermore Valley to oversee the harvesting of his wheat field; he consulted with astronomers on proposals for a larger observatory; he worked on water company plans for a large receiving reservoir in the Highland Park area; he studied the latest blue prints of his sheltering home; and he changed many of his investments. One day in early November he drove himself until after midnight. His frail frame overtaxed, the next day he was back in bed at Remi's house. This time he didn't get up.[3]

For the next eight weeks it was steadily downhill. Anthony knew that he would not recover; but his mind was clear, and he continued to make his final business and charitable decisions from his bed. On November 7, he dictated a codicil to his will. Finally, Mary Ann and Ellen returned from the East. By the end of December, Anthony made no more decisions. He was unconscious much of the time. On Friday afternoon, January 6, 1888, during a lucid momement, he assured his grieving family and close friends that he was not suffering and bade an affectionate farewell to his loved ones. At 8:15 that evening Oakland's greatest benefactor died quietly in his sleep. His death was officially due to cirrhosis of the liver, complicated by dropsy, but his hyperactivity and overwork during his 38 years in

California were contributing factors.[4]

For many days the press had been preparing the public for Chabot's death, but the sight of the flags at half-mast on Saturday morning shocked the community. Newspapers on both sides of the bay ran long obituaries eulogizing Oakland's Water King. Monday, January ninth, was a day of mourning. The city's schools and most businesses were closed, and from early morning thousands of people packed the route from the First Congregational Church to Mountain View Cemetery to pay their last respects to the shy little man who had so greatly improved their city.

Chabot lay in state over the weekend in the parlor of his home. Family services were held there at 11:00 a.m. Monday. Reverend J.K. McLean of the First Congregational Church officiated. The casket was then escorted to the church by employees of the Contra Costa Water Company who were joined halfway along the route to the church by a Masonic group. Once the casket was inside the church, the Live Oak Masonic Lodge, #61, conducted the ceremony. Reverend McLean read the scriptures and gave a stirring eulogy to the packed church. The mourners represented almost every organization in Oakland. Anthony's oldest friends, Tubbs, Shattuck, Eastland, and Pierce were among the pall bearers. The church was filled with the most exquisite and unique floral pieces. The Board of Education presented a floral model of Chabot Observatory made with white roses, heliotrope, hyacinths, camellias, and chrysanthemums.

The procession from 12th and Webster to the cemetery was the longest in Oakland's history up to that time, and possibly to the present. The procession was led by a police guard followed by the Fifth Regiment Band and a marching unit with arms reversed. The Grand Army of the Republic, the Society of California Pioneers, the Masonic Order, and the Trustees of the Hebrew

Congregation were also among the many organizations in the procession. The marchers were followed by mourners in 35 hired hacks (all that were available in Oakland and Alameda), followed by dozens of private buggies and carriages.

The bell at Mountain View Cemetery tolled solemnly as the long line of marchers and mourners sadly passed under the arched entrance. Anthony's friends gathered around a central grassy plot where the Masonic burial service was conducted. At the conclusion of the service the casket was placed temporarily in the private vault of Hiram Tubbs, pending the final preparation of Chabot's plot which Anthony had purchased years before, and on which he had placed a tall, granite obelisk. On January 19th Chabot's casket was quietly removed from his friend's vault. It was placed in his own tomb on a grassy hillside under his monument which was simply inscribed, "Sacred to the Menory of Antoine Chabot, Died January 6, 1888, 74 years, 4 months, 10 days."[5]

Epilogue

Chabot's Will

Chabot left an estate estimated at the time of his death at over $1,400,000, mostly in securities, plus mining properties and other interests of undetermined values. This was a very large amount in 1888. (About $1,000,000 of his assets were in Contra Costa Water Company securities, which were to depreciate greatly by the end of the century.) His creditors claimed about $100,000, and he left nearly $100,000 to his major charities—the Ladies' Relief Society, the Women's Sheltering Home, and the Board of Education (for the observatory).

The rest of the will dealt mainly with his family. It is obvious that Anthony and Mary Ann were estranged when he drew up the document in June, 1887. He made a point of inviting Ellen and any family she might have, and Remi and his family to join him upon their deaths in the Chabot plot in Mountain View. No such invitation was extended to Mary Ann. He only bequeathed his wife Contra Costa Water Company securities then valued at $110,000, plus $5,000 in gold coin. She had to share with Ellen, Remi, and Emelie any residual amount. She would not go hungry in her fine home (which was apparently in her name), but her share of the estate was small in proportion to other bequests.

Anthony originally had willed Ellen about $700,000 in securities. But shortly before his death he deeded over to her all of his valuable farmland and much of his urban real estate. He then changed his will and left her $500,000 in securities.

He willed the additional $200,000 in securities to Remi and Emelie for the care they had taken of him during his last illness. Altogether Remi and Emelie received about $300,000 in securities, plus all his interests in the Vallejo Water Works, the Pioneer Pulp Company, the Cranberry Company, and several lesser investments. Thus Remi and Emelie received over three times Mary Ann's share.

Chabot's sister, Modiste, in Montreal, was given $14,000, although no other siblings were so favored. Many notes he held against individuals were generously cancelled. Ellen, Hiram, and Remi were executors. The estate was not fully settled until early in the next century.[6]

The Water Company

Anthony's Contra Costa Water company was managed for the next eleven years by Henry Pierce, during which time its name symbolized the zenith of corporate ruthlessness. About 1890 William Dingee, a local realtor, set up a rival water company which supplied Oakland with pure water from local hillside springs and wells near Alvarado. There followed a decade of vicious corporate warfare. Henry fought like a demon. One night he shut off the street valves of his competitor's customers, and announced that Dingee's system had failed. Another night he punched holes in his rival's flumes in the Alvarado tide flats. The next morning Dingee's customers had salt water. A Dingee Reservoir was mysteriously dynamited, flooding a section of Oakland. Henry cut his water rates to the bone. But he lost the water war. Dingee (who was no angel!) merged the two ruined companies under the Contra Costa name and ousted Pierce and his cohorts. Henry died, at 75, in San Francisco in January, 1903. The corporate rogue also had an impressive funeral, but nothing like Anthony's. The Contra Costa Water Company sent him a wreath of cypress leaves and pink roses. But President Dingee must have been too busy to attend.[7]

Chabot's water company died unlamented in 1906. It was

followed by two unsuccessful private water companies. In the 1920's the East Bay Municipal Utility District was founded. Although it brought Oakland plentiful water from the Sierras in 1929, at this writing Oakland is once again in the throes of a severe water shortage.[8]

Mary Ann

For nearly 17 years Mary Ann lived in the seclusion of her home, surrounded by her books, with only Ellen for company. She very seldom attended social activities, and invited very few guests to her home. Her life continued to revolve around Ellen whom she loved dearly. This love was reciprocated, and Ellen remained in her family home and comforted Mary Ann during the stepmother's declining years.

Although Mary Ann never traveled again after her husband's death, shortly before she died, she planned one last rail trip. Anthony did not want her in his tomb, and she would not even rest in the same cemetery with him. She arranged with her brothers to bring her body back to Lynn.

After a long illness, the Water King's unhappy widow died on November 12, 1904. Two of her brothers, Edward and Nathaniel, were at her bedside. In her will she requested a "...Christian burial, with due repect to my station in life." This request was respected; she had two funeral services.

On November 15, Reverend C.R. Brown conducted a Congregational service in the parlor of her home. There were many flowers, and a few mourners. A quartet sang "Nearer My God to Thee." Her body was temporarily placed in a vault in Mountain View, while her brothers and Ellen filed her will for probate. Ellen, at her own request, was willed only the house and her stepmother's personal possessions. Mary Ann's relatives in Lynn split about $160,000.

On Sunday afternoon, November 27, Mary Ann lay in her brother Edward's parlor. Her three brothers, a sister, and a crowd of grieving old friends attended her second Congregational funeral service. Finally, over two weeks after her death, Mary Ann (Bacheller) Chabot, age 71, was laid to rest in the family plot in Lynn's Pine Grove Cemetery.[9]

Remi

Remi had worked at his brother's side for 38 years. Although he had resigned from the Contra Costa Water Company when Pierce became president, he took Anthony's seat as trustee in 1888 and vainly tried to soften Pierce's policies. But in March of 1890, Remi fell ill. Like his brother, he had a liver ailment. He was taken to San Francisco for treatment and died there in the Baldwin Hotel. The funeral service was held at his home which was packed with friends and relatives. But neither Mary Ann nor Ellen were listed among the mourners. Henry Pierce was head pall bearer. The casket was conveyed to the Chabot plot in Mountain View. At 61, Remi was once again at his brother's side.[10]

Emelie

Emelie Chabot, a beautiful woman until her death, continued on with her life much as before. Sustained by Remi's personal fortune, plus Anthony's liberal bequests, Emelie was a leader of East Bay society. She continued to donate the Water King's fortune to deeds of charity and to conduct philanthropic institutions. She was president of the Fabiola Hospital Association to the day of her death, and continued her activities in the Ladies' Relief Society and the Women's Sheltering Home. As time went on, Emelie immersed herself in the Women's Congress of the Pacific Coast, an early feminist organization that campaigned for the right of women to vote. She also headed several volunteer groups at St.

Francis de Sales Church in Oakland.

Meanwhile, Emelie brought up her four daughters who were between nine and 19 at the time of their father's death. Emelie saw to it that they had the proper education and met the right persons in society. At various times between 1889 and 1902 all four girls visited Europe. They all married men from prominent families and followed their mother as leaders of society.[11]

The fashionable residential district began to move from the flatlands to the foothills, and in 1910 Emelie built a beautiful home on Perry Street looking down on Grand Avenue. The home remained in the family for many decades, but Emelie had little time to enjoy it. By 1914 she was bedridden from an accident. On June 25, 1916, she died at Fabiola Hospital.

Before her death Emelie requested that she be buried beside Remi in Mountain View, despite the fact that the cemetery was not Catholic. The strong-willed woman defied convention. Her funeral service was conducted by a Catholic priest at her home, but her interment was without the usual rites. She lies today beside her husband and brother-in-law. Two of her daughters, Henrietta and Josephine, lie near her.[12]

Ellen

Ellen Hasty Chabot, better known as "Nellie," was 39 when her step-mother died. After that she led a fabulous life.

Although after her father's death, Ellen was a wealthy 22-year-old heiress, with almost unlimited income, she elected to remain quietly at home with Mary Ann for 17 years. As an executor of her father's estate, a member of the board of the sheltering home, and a major stockholder in several corporations, Ellen did have occasions to leave the house and meet people. But these were generally business people, her father's former associates. She seems to have had no further formal education after the semester in New York in 1887, but, like Mary Ann, she read extensively at home. Mary Ann's isolation from society discouraged Ellen from accepting social engagements. Only toward the end of her stepmother's life, when Ellen was in her mid-thirties, did the heiress begin "going out."

Ellen seems to have accepted her stepmother's influence without complaint. She loved her as a mother, and possibly she wanted to make up for years of neglect and loneliness that Mary Ann had suffered from Ellen's father. [13]

After Mary Ann's death, Ellen continued to live in the big house by the Lake, but her lifestyle changed. She soon showed that she had exquisite and expensive tastes. Her wardrobe was in the height of fashion. She still loved books and added to her stepmother's extensive library. She had book plates specially designed and engraved by George H. Gihon of San Francisco. A wreath, with two fish at the bottom, encircled: "EX LIBRIS, Ellen H. Chabot." She also liked fine foods and wines. Like her father, Ellen loved beautiful landscaping and gardens.

Ellen traveled extensively, and in April, 1909, apparently visited her mother's grave at Standish. Shocked by its condition, she provided a fund for the perpetual care of the Hasty plot, which is still immaculately tended.[14]

East Bay society had assumed that Ellen was destined to become a spinster. There were few, if any, eligible unmarried men in her age group. But Ellen fell in love with a most ineligible 55-year-old man. He was divorced with three children. But he was one of the richest men in the Bay Area.

Henry Bothin was the President of the Judson Manufacturing Company which Ellen's father helped organize and in which Ellen held a sizable block of stock. Bothin, who had a palatial residence in Ross, Marin County, was also one of the largest land owners in San Francisco. He was a well-known club man and a prominent member of Oakland's Claremont Country Club. The romance was very low key, almost secret. On June 3 they applied for a license at the Alameda County Court House, and that afternoon they were married in Ellen's home by Reverend Wirt of the First Congregational Church. Only six persons were in attendance. Several days later the press finally learned of the event which had combined two of the Bay Area's larger fortunes.[15]

Ellen soon sold her lakeside home, and had little more to do with Oakland. In 1914 the couple began work on a 20-room home in Montecito, near Santa Barbara. Called Piranhurst, the structure followed the style of the early Italian Renaissance. There were beautifully landscaped terraces, conservatories, and a glass-covered swimming pool. There was also a complete outdoor theater, with a velvety lawn used for a stage and cypress hedges that formed the wings and the backdrop. The estate also contained many art objects that Ellen acquired on her trips to Europe.

Upon her marriage Ellen became a stepmother and later a stepgrandmother. As she had no children of her own, Ellen, like Mary Ann, enjoyed the role. She lavishly and frequently entertained at Piranhurst. Despite a heart problem during the last 30 years of her life, she enjoyed life to its fullest until shortly before her death.

Henry Bothin died in 1923 leaving an $8,000,000 estate. Ellen had inherited her father's business acumen, and remained active until her very old age in her late husband's business affairs and charities. Her last business activity was as president of the Bothin Real Estate Company in San Francisco.

Ellen's weak heart finally gave out. The Water King's daughter by his beloved Ellen died at Santa Barbara on February 10, 1965. She was 99.[16]

Endnotes

There is a dearth of readily available information covering Chabot's life. It appears that for some unknown reason, possibly to cover either his financial manipulations, or his unhappy marriage, most of Chabot's personal records have been deliberately destroyed.

While doing research in 1948 for my master's thesis on the early Oakland water supply, I received a letter from Ellen Chabot Bothin, Chabot's daughter. She stated that "...[Chabot's] executors, who probably destroyed all his papers , are individuals long since dead and...a record of his affairs was probably not kept. As far as I know, no letters, diaries, or other documents were preserved by anyone."

As Ellen herself was one of the three executors (and was still very much alive), it is obvious that she knew that his papers were destroyed. I received much the same reply in a letter from Josephine Chabot Dieckmann, Remi's daughter, and in an interview with Mrs. Dieckmann's son.

Chabot's business papers suffered a similar fate. In 1899 at the end of the "Water War," which is mentioned in the Epilogue, all the business records of the Contra Costa Water Company were burned.

Consequently, this story of Anthony Chabot relies heavily upon newspaper accounts, government documents, and third party recollections of the man. My extensively documented thesis, which is the basis of chapters 7, 8, 10, and 11, also is based on similar source material.

Abbreviations

The following references will be frequently cited in these notes. They will be identified by the shortened citations and abbreviations.

Burgess Thesis—Sherwood D. Burgess, "Early History of the Oakland Water Supply, 1850-1876" (M.A. Thesis, University of California, Berkeley, 1948).

Chab. Sch.—Children of the Sixth Grade, Gertrude Smith, Teacher, *Life of Anthony Chabot* (Oakland: Anthony Chabot School, 1930). Ellen Chabot Bothin (Chabot's daughter) was the principal source for this book. She provided many anecdotes of Chabot's life.

Mem. Rec.—California Society of Pioneers, Memorial Record Vol.13, "Antoine Chabot," (San Francisco:1888).

Pierce Pap.—Pierce Family Papers, The Kay Clegg collection, Santa Rosa, Calif.

Oak. Dir., S.F. Dir.—City Directories: Beginning in 1850 in San Francisco and in 1869 in Oakland, directories were published approximately once a year. Although publishers changed and full titles varied, collections are shelved by date.

Newspapers: Although the details of the mastheads changed over the years, the principal names of the papers remained the same. "Obit" (obituary) will be used in place of "7 Jan. 1888," (the day after Chabot's death) in newspaper citations. Example: *Times*, Obit.

Alta	*Alta California*
Chron.	*San Francisco Chronicle*
Enq.	*The Oakland Enquirer*
Times	*The [Oakland] Morning Times*
Trib.	*Oakland Daily Evening Tribune*

Chapter 1

1. Chab. Sch. 11; (Ellen Chabot claims that the Chabot family goes back to the "original colonizer of Canada, Admiral Phillippe de Chabot;" Cyprien Tanquay, *Genealogique de Familles Canadiennes,* (Montreal: 1886), 2:593, traces Chabots in Quebec back to 1639.

2. Mem. Rec. 370; *Enq.,* Obit.; Chab. Sch. ll-12; Vera Holmes, *A History of the Americas* (New York: Ronald Press, 1950), 479-93.

3. Mem. Rec. 370.

4. Dorothie Bobbe, "Philip Hone's New York," *American Heritage* VIII:5 (August, 1957): 12.

5. Chab. Sch. 14.

6. Mem. Rec. 371.; *Enq.,* Obit.; Stephen F. Miller, *Recollections of Newbern Fifty Years Ago* (Columbus, Ga.: 1873), 33, (Typewritten Copy, Craven-Pamlico-Carteret Library, New Bern, N.C.); *Encyclopaedia Britannica,* 14th ed., s.v. "Leather."

7. Ross Robertson, *History of the American Economy* (New York: Harcourt, 1964), Chapter 6, Map, p.137; See standard textbooks on the ante-bellum South and Mississippi Valley.

8. *Enq.,* Obit.; Mem. Rec. 371; That he put down no roots and acquired no land in the valley is indicated by answers to letters from the author to court houses and libraries of major cities in the valley. As they uncovered no public records of Chabot, he must have made money through trade and shrewd investments. He had money to invest in a steamboat at Louisville, he was prepared to build a tannery upon his return to St. Hyacinthe, and before he sailed from New Orleans he had money to finance his brother's trip to California.

9. *Enq., Obit.;* Mem. Rec. 371.

10. Mem. Rec. 371.

Chapter 2

1. Mem. Rec. 371.

2. Mem. Rec. 371.; *Enq.,* Obit.

3. Mem. Rec. 371.; *Enq.,* Obit.

4. Mem. Rec. 371–372.

5. C.W. Haskins, *The Argonauts of California* (New York: Fords, Howard, and Hulbert, 1890), 481.; Mem. Rec. 372.

6. Mem. Rec. 372; *Enq.,* Obit.

7. Octavius T. Howe, *Argonauts of '49; History of Emigrant Companies from Massachusetts, 1849-1850* (Cambridge: Harvard U. Press, 1923), 26.

8. Mem. Rec. 372; *Enq.*, Obit; David Lavender, *California: Land of New Beginnings* (New York: Harper and Row, 1972), 167.

9. *Alta*, 1 Mar., 2 Apr. 1849, "Shipping Notices," (Arrivals in S.F. of *California* and *Oregon.*); *Alta*, 21 June 1849, (Arrival of bark *Equator* on June 16, 81 days out of Panama [sailed March 27 at the time Chabot would have reached Panama].)

10. *Alta*, 19 July 1849, "Wed. July 18, New Gren. Brig, *Josephine*, Mantilla, 90 days from Panama, 80 passengers." (This was the only arrival listed on the date Chabot arrived in S.F.)

11. Mem. Rec. 372.

12. John Caughey, *California* (New York: Prentice Hall, 1946), 358; *Sketch Book, Napa, Sonoma, and Mendocino Counties* (CHS Lib.), 50.

Chapter 3

1. Mem. Rec. 372; *Trib.*, Obit.; *Alta*, 26 July 1849, "U.S. Mail Packet Lines;" "The California Recollections of Caspar Hopkins," *California Historical Society Quarterly* 25:2 (June 1946): 103, an excellent description of a voyage up the Sacramento River.

2. *Alta*, 26 July 1849, "Sam Brannan & Co." ad.; David Comstock, *Gold Diggers and Camp Followers* (Grass Valley: Bonanza Press, 1982), 231, 265.

3. William Chamberlain, *History of Yuba County* (Oakland: Thompson and West, 1879 [1970 reprint]), 88; Earl Ramey, "Beginnings of Marysville," *CHSQ* 15:1 (1936): 20; *Colville's Marysville Directory* (San Francisco: Monson-Valentine 1855), iii.

4. *The Little Town of Rough & Ready* (Rough & Ready [CA]: Chamber of Commerce, Undated Pamphlet), 2.

5. H.L. Wells, *History of Nevada County* (Oakland: Thompson and West, 1880 [1970 reprint.]), 53, 78, 79.; Edwin F. Bean, *History and Directory of Nevada County* (Nevada City: 1867), 10-13; H.P. Davis, *Gold Rush Days in Nevada City* (Nevada City: Berliner & McGinnis, 1948), includes, "Historical Map of Nevada City Compiled ...by H.S. Bradley 1869—Edw.C. Uren 1932 and drawn by H.P. Davis 1948".

6. Philip Ross May, *Origins of Hydraulic Mining in California* (Oakland: Holmes Book Company, 1970), 40–41; Davis' map labels Buckeye Ravine in present Nevada City, "1852-3 first steps in hydraulic mining." Chabot took those first steps in 1852. Other sources, quoted later, also place Chabot in Buckeye Ravine or on Buckeye Hill in Nevada City. May, *Origins*, 67-70, quotes a fanciful tale by George Poore in 1947, which places Chabot on a Buckeye Hill near Red Dog, a few miles east of Nevada City. This story is too full of obvious errors (e.g., Chabot came overland to California in 1852, and worked Buckeye Hill for several years thereafter) to be taken seriously.

7. *Brown and Dallison's, Nevada Directory*. (San Francisco: Brown and Dallison, 1856) 19, 20; Comstock, *Gold Diggers*, 237.

8. Mem. Rec. 372.

9. *Times*, 30 Mar. 1890, (Remi's obituary. All Oakland and S.F. papers of same date agree Remi arrived in Calif. in 1850.)

10. Comstock, *Gold Diggers*, 383; Wells, *History*, 79-82; Bean *History*, 12, 13; Brown and Dallison, *Directory*, 22-34.

11. Wells, *History*, 79; Comstock, *Gold Diggers*, 332-335; May, *Origins*, 34; Brown and Dallison, *Directory*, 26.

12. Chab.Sch. 22; Mem. Rec. 372; May, *Origins*, 26-27, 36.

13. "Anthony Chabot. The Inventor of Hydraulic Mining," *Nevada City Herald*, copied in *Trib*. 11 Feb. 1888? (Clipping in Chabot Observatory archives.)

14. May, *Origins*, 26-39; Bean *History*, 61-62; Wells, *History*, 179.

15. W.W. Kallenberger, "The French in Nevada County's Early History," *Nevada County Historical Society* 8:2, (Mar. 1954): unpaged; Erwin Gudde, *California Gold Camps* (Berkeley: U.C. Press, 1975), 50; August J. Bowie, *A Practical Treatise on Hydraulic Mining in California* (New York: Van Nostrand, 1885), 48-50; "Hittell's Scraps," 3:88 (Bancroft Lib.); Nevada City Historical Library, Box 36-M, "E.E.Matteson;" *Wells, History*, 179; *Bean's History*, 62; May, 41.

Chapter 4

1. Mem. Rec. 372; Fariss and Smith, *History of Plumas, Lassen, and Sierra Counties* (San Francisco: Farris & Smith, 1882), 290-291.

2. All legal documents recorded in Sierra County use "Anthony" or "A." We have no such records from Nevada County as the courthouse burned in 1856.

3. *Chron., Trib., Times, Enq.*, Obits; Map, *County of Sierra*, (1867), Ban. Lib.; Gudde, *Gold Camps*, (Camps are described alphabetically.); Sunset Books, *Gold Rush Country*, (Menlo Park: Lane Publishing Co., 1972), 10, 118, 119.

4. Sierra County Records, Mortgages: A:121, Oct. 22, 1853, A:262, May 11,1854.

5. There are no recorded documents detailing the origins of the sawmill partnership. But documents cited in notes 7 and 8 below contain much information concerning the mills.

6. May, *Origins*, 25.

7. Chab. Sch. 23-24; Sierra Cty, Deeds: A:227, Sept. 1, 1854; Mort: A:262, Sept. 1, 1854.

8. Sierra Cty, Morts: B:494, May 26, 1856, A:262 (Release written on original Mort.), July 15, 1856.

9. May, *Origins*, 22. (This also explains why there are no original deeds to the land on which Chabot built his sawmills.)

10. Sierra Cty, Morts: A:270, Sept. 7, 1854, A:271, Sept. 9, 1854, B:15, May 12, 1855, B:688, July 15, 1856, B:270, July 15, 1856, B:713, Aug. 1, 1856; Contracts: AB:121, Jan. 15, 1855.

11. Haskins, *Argonauts,* 481. (There were two J. Thompsons aboard the *Galveston.* There is no positive evidence that any of Chabot's California associates sailed with him.)

12. Sierra Cty, Water Claims: A:97, Mar. 30, 1855.

13. Sierra Cty, Personal Mort: A:368, Oct. 30, 1857. (Remi, a miner living in St. Louis, loans $3,000 against a ditch and a sawmill.)

14. The effects of hydraulic mining on both the economy and the environment is discussed in most standard works on California history.

15. Yuba County, Mort: 4:222 and 4:435, Dec. 26, 1854; Sierra Cty, Contracts: AB: 121, Jan. 15, 1855; Chamberlain, *Hist. Yuba,* 136.

16. Colville, *Dir.,* iii, xx, 15, 85, 86.

17. Ibid. 13.

18. Ibid. 41; Chamberlain, *Hist. Yuba,* 50.

19. Mem. Rec. 373; Yuba Cty, Deeds: 9:449, Aug. 11, 1855, 12:134, Nov. 11, 1857, 13:414, Nov, 12, 1859, 13:447, Oct. 4, 1859; Mort: 5:199, July 10, 1856.

20. Yuba Cty, Deeds: 10:588, July 11, 1856; Colville, *Dir.,* 15 (Calif. Steam Nav. Co.); Sierra Cty, Mort: B:668, 670, July, 15, 1856, "...Anthony Chabot of...San Francisco..."

Chapter 5

1. James P. Delgado, "The Humblest Cottage Can in a Short Time Afford ...Pure and Sparkling Water. Early Efforts to Solve Gold Rush San Francisco's Water Shortage," *Pacific Historian* 26:3 (Fall 1982): 26-30; Delgado, "The Bensley Water System...," (National Park Service: 1980), 1-3, (A typewritten, longer version of the above excellent article, in Ban. Lib.); Doris Muscatine, *Old San Francisco,* (New York: Putnam, 1975), 237.

2. *S.F. Dir.,* (1856), s.v. Railroad House; (1858), s.v. Chabot, A.

3. San Francisco City and County, "Great Register, Supplemental List," August 1868.

4. John R Freeman, *On the Proposed Use of ... the Hetch Hetchy ...* (S.F.: Rincon Publishing, 1912), 386; Delgado, *Humblest,* 31-32; Muscatine, *Old S.F.,* 237; "The Mountain Lake Folly," *Call,* 31 May 1893; "Pamphlets on San Francisco," vol 2, Ban. Lib., (Mountain Lake Co.); Undated clippings, CHS Lib., "Mountain Lake Water Co." (Apr. 1862?).

5. *San Francisco Water,* (Spring Valley Water Co. Publication, 1922-1930), July 1926; *S.F. Dir.,* (1861) s.v. S.V. Water Co.; *S.F. Bulletin,* 20 May 1857; Freeman, *Hetch Hetchy,* 386.

6. G.W. Sullivan, *Early Days in California* (San Francisco: Enterprise Publishers, 1888), I, 185-187; Bancroft Manuscript, C-D 909, Biographical Sketch, John Bensley.

7. Mem. Rec. 373; *Call,* 31 May 1893.

8. *S.F. Water,* Aug. 1929, Jan. 1922; *S.F. Dir.,* (July, 1859), s.v. S.F. City W.W.

9. Delgado, *Humblest,* 32-33; Delgado, *Bensley,* (ms), 4.

10. *Charter of the San Francisco City Water Works,* (San Francisco: Towne & Bacon, 1860), 11. (Booklet also includes Supervisors'Orders #46, Aug. 6, 1957; #65, May 28, 1958; #92, Jan. 22, 1959; #172, Aug. 29, 1959.

11. *Charter,* Order #48, 22-27.

12. S.F., "Great Register," Aug. 1868.

13. Delgado, *Humblest,* 32-33; *S.F. Dir.,* (July, 1859), s.v. S.F. City W.W.; For tunnel through Fort Point see, Public Utilities Commission, S.F...., *San Francisco Water and Power* (April, 1935), 2; *Trib.,* Obit.; Chab. Sch. 31; A longer tunnel was bored in 1862 see, *Bulletin,* 22 Aug. 1862, quoted in Delgado, *Humblest,* 35.

14. *Charter,* Order #65, 28-30.

15. Delgado, *Humblest,* 33-35; *S.F. Dir.,* (July, 1859), s.v. S.F. City W.W.; *S.F. Water,* Jan. 1922, quote from *Alta,* 18 June 1858.

16. *Charter,* Order #172, 31-35.

17. *S.F. Dir.,* (July, 1860, Sept. 1861, Sept. 1862), s.v. S.F. City W.W.

18. S.F.C.W.W., *Rules and Regulations...* (S.F.: Pamphlets, 1858, 1860, 1861); Delgado, *Humblest,* 35; *Bulletin,* 9 Dec. 58.

19. *S.F. Water,* Oct. 1922, Aug. 1929; *S.F. Dir.,* (1861 and 1862), s.v. S.F. City W.W., Spring Valley Water Co.

20. Association of Engineering Societies, *The Water Supply of San Francisco,* (1908), 20-24, 87; Freeman, *Hetch Hetchy,* 386-387; *S.F. Dir.,* (July 1861, Sept. 1862, Dec. 1865), s.v. S.F.City W.W., Spring Valley Water Co.; *S.F. Water,* July 1924, July 1926, Aug. 1929; Delgado, *Humblest,* 36-37.

21. *Alta,* 4 May 1861, 15 Jan. 1862; *Bulletin,* 15 Jan. 1862; *Evening Journal,* 20 Jan. 1862. (See water supply clippings CHS Lib.).

22. *Mirror,* 21, 28 Jan. 1862; *S.F. Water,* Oct. 1922; *S.F. Dir.,* (Oct. 1864), s.v. S.F. City W.W., Spring Valley Water Co.; (Dec. 1865), s.v. Spring Valley Water Co.

23. *S.F. Dir.,* (Sept. 1962), (Oct. 1863), (Oct. 1864), (Dec. 1865), s.v. Bensley, J, Chabot, A, J, R, Von Schmidt, A., Spring Valley Water Co.

23. *S.F. Dir.,* (Sept. 1962), (Oct. 1863), (Oct. 1864), (Dec. 1865), s.v. Bensley, J, Chabot.

Chapter 6

1. Chab. Sch., 30; *Trib.,* Obit.; *S.F. Dir.,* (Sept. 1862), (Oct. 1863), (Oct. 1864), no listings for Chabot, A; (Dec.1, 1865), s.v. Chabot, A, cites res. and office.

2. *Trib.,* 16 Jan. 1903, (Sermon at Pierce's funeral.); *Enq.,* 14 Jan. 1903; *Chron.,* 14 Jan. 1903; Letter, Kay Clegg to author, Sept. 6, 1986.; Ltr., Robert Hotle to author, Apr. 17, 1985; Pierce Pap, "Ltrs., Marshall to sister Anne, Dec. 30, 1853, Dec. 5, 1858."; York County [Maine], "Supreme Judicial Records" (1863), 20:305, (H.Pierce in Biddeford, Aug.3, 1861, away in 1862 and early 1863, stood trial in Biddeford, Aug. 1863); S.F. *Dir.,* (1861), s.v. Pierce, H., no res. listing.

3. Ltr., Kay Clegg to author, Sept. 6, 1986, (Pierces owned property in Wisconsin); Chab. Sch., 33; *Trib.,* Obit.; *Encyclopaedia Britannica,* 14th ed., s.v. "Milwaukee."; Robert Wells, *This is Milwaukee* (New York: Doubleday, 1970), 112, 114; Ltr., "Milwaukee, Supt. of Water Works to author, Dec. 8, 1947.

4. Mody Boatright, *Tales from the Derrick Floor* (New York: Doubleday, 1970), 3, 243; Anthony Sampson, *The Seven Sisters* (New York: Viking Press, 1975), 19; Richard Walton, *Power of Oil* (New York: Seabury Press, 1977), 29-32.

5. Chab. Sch. 33; *Trib.,* Obit.

6. Portland [Maine] Water Company, *Water Supply, Rates...* (Portland: 1881), 13-18, (Maine Hist. Soc.).

7. Personal visit to Maine by author, 1987; Telephone interview with Mylice Waite, curator of Red Church, Standish, 1987; Town of Standish, "Record of Births," 1:23; Albert Sears, "Early Families of Standish, Maine," (Typewritten MS, ca. 1983), 78.

8. Portland Water Co., 18; Ltr., Portland Water District to author, Nov. 17, 1947.

9. Ltr., Kay Clegg to author, quotes from Ltr., William to niece, Aug. 9, 1871, (William in Boston on business for Chabot); Pierce Pap., "Marshall Pierce memoirs," 1881; Author searched public records of Cumberland and York counties and in Maine Archives, but uncovered no deeds, mortgages, law suits, etc. of A. Chabot.

10. Pierce Pap., "Ltr., Henry P. to sister, Ann," Mar. 25, 1865, (mentions Chabot's interest in a stout girl at Lynn); "Ltr., William P. to sister," June 18, 1866, ("[Chabot] Speaks very kindly of you all. Lynn people have a kind place in his heart I think.")

11. Maine Historical Society, Portland, "Standish Clippings."

12. Maine Hist. Soc., "Hasty Clippings," Oct. 3, 1899; Sears, "Early Families," 78; Census Record, 1870, Cumberland County, Standish, June 27, 1870, (Maine Archives); Town of Standish, "Record of Marriages," 1:353; phone conversation with Mylice White, curator of Red Church, Standish.

13. Town of Standish, "Records of Death, 1864-1867," 6; "Records of Births," 1:59.

14. *S.F. Dir.,* Dec. 1, 1865, s.v. Chabot, A.; Maine Census Record, 1870 (author's visit to graveyard).

Chapter 7

1. *S.F. Dir.,* (Dec. 1, 1865), s.v. Chabot,A., Chabot, R.

2. Mem. Rec. 374; Charles Coleman, *P.G. & E. of California,* (Glendale: Arthur Clark Co., 1959), 23; Douglas S. Watson, "To California Through Texas and Mexico...[Eastland papers]," *CHSQ* 18:2, (June, 1939): 99-100.

3. Burgess Thesis, 6-8; Beth Bagwell, *Oakland...,* (Novato: Presidio Press, 1982), 3-53; *Historical Atlas of Alameda County,* (Oakland: Thompson and West, 1878), [Fresno: Valley Publishers, 1976 reprint], 17-20.

4. Burgess Thesis, 16-17; Thompson and West, 19-21.

5. Coleman, *P.G. & E.,* 38-41; Bagwell, *Oakland,* 142; *Oak. Dir.,* (1870), 40.

6. Burgess Thesis, 3-6, map p. 4; Thompson and West, 17; Bagwell, *Oakland,* 12-13.

7. Burgess Thesis, 14-16.

8. Ibid. 17.

9. Ibid. 17-19.

10. Ibid. 39-40.

11. Ibid. 40. 42, 43; *Oakland Daily News,* 8 Apr. 1870.

12. Burgess Thesis, 41.

13. Ibid. 41.

14. Ibid. 42.

15. Ibid. 43.

16. Ibid. 44.; *Oakland Evening Transcript,* 18 May 1868.

Chapter 8

1. Burgess Thesis, 35.

2. Ibid. 44-46.

3. *S.F. Dir.,* (Oct. 1868), s.v. Pierce, H.; Pierce Pap., "Ltr. William to Sister," June 18, 1866.

4. *S.F. Dir.,* (Dec. 1869), s.v. Chabot,A, no listing; *Oak. Dir.,* (1869), s.v. Chabot,A, Eureka Hotel.

5. "W.F. Boardman," *Trib.,* 5 June 1886.

6. Burgess Thesis, 47-48.

7. Ibid. 34.

8. Ibid. 48-49.

9. Ibid. 49.

10. Ibid. 49-50.

11. Ibid. 50-51.

12. Ibid. 52-53.

13. Ibid. 52, 54.

14. Ibid. 51-52.

15. Ibid. 56.

16. Ibid. 50, 69.

17. *Oak. Dir.,* (1870), s.v. Chabot,A (Pres. C.C. Water Works, res. S.F.).

18. *Trib.,* "Illustrated Annual Edition," (Jan. 1890,), 6, (picture, Remi).

19. Bancroft Lib., Chabot File, "Family [Remi Chabot] Bible," "Marriage License, Remi and Emelie."; Remi Obits., *Chron.,* 30 Mar. 1890, *Times,* 30 Mar., 1 Apr. 1890, *Trib.,* 29 Mar. 1890, *Alta,* 30 Mar. 1890; Emelie, Obits., *Chron.,* 26 Mar. 1916, *Trib.,* 26 Mar. 1916; *Trib.,* 25 May 1952.

20. *Oak. Dir.,* (1870), s.v. Chabot, R.

21. Photographed by author.

22. City of Lynn, Mass., "Marriage Certificate, Anthony Chabot- Mary Ann Bacheller," July 28, 1870; *Lynn Semi-weekly Reporter,* 30 July 1870.

23. *Daily News,* 11 Aug. 1870.

24. *Oak. Dir.* (June 1873), s.v. Chabot, R.

25. Contra Costa Water Company, "Certificate of Increase in Capital Stock," Oct. 15, 1870 (E. Chabot, Secretary); Pacific County [Washington], "Deeds," C:528, (Anthony Chabot, President, Emilie M. Chabot, Secretary, Pacific Cranberry Company of Oakland.); Pacific County [Washington], "Deeds," C:52.

Chapter 9

1. *A Century of Service...* (San Jose: Bicentennial Commission, 1977), 2, 3, 39, 40; *Historical Atlas Santa Clara...* (Oakland: Thompson and West, 1876), 18.

2. Clyde Arbuckle, *History of San Jose* (San Jose: Smith & McKay, 1986), 505.

3. Leslie Parks, "A History of the San Jose Water Company" (Master's Thesis, San Jose State College, 1983), 14-17.

4. *Century,* 39-40; Arbuckle, 505; San Jose Water Works, *A Wealth of Good Water* (San Jose: 1937), 21-22, includes picture of tanks; Parks Thesis, 25.

5. Frederic Hall, *History of San Jose* (San Francisco: A.L. Bancroft, 1871), 305; *Nine Men and 100 years of Water History* (San Jose: S.J. Water Works, 1967), 10 unnumbered leaves, "Donald McKenzie"; Parks Thesis, 25-28; *Century,* 40; Arbuckle, 505.

6. Parks Thesis, 29-34; Arbuckle, 506; *Hist. Atlas,* 15; Arbuckle, 506; *A Wealth,* 22; Hall, 306; *Nine Men,* "Donald McKenzie."

7. *Nine Men,* "Nathaniel H.A. Mason;" Hall, 306; Arbuckle, 506; Parks Thesis, 29.

8. Parks Thesis, 34-40; *Century,* 40; *Hist. Atlas,* 15.

9. Mem. Rec. 375.

10.*Nine Men,* "Edward Williams."

11. Tom Gregory, *History of Solano and Napa Counties* (Los Angeles: Historic Record Co., 1912), 749; *Solano and Napa Counties Directory* (Sacramento: County Directory Pub. Co. 1871), 129, 290.

12. Gregory, 86-94.

13. Frank Leach, *Recollections of a Newspaper Man* (San Francisco: Levinson, 1917), 157; Ernest Wichels, "Pages from the Past, Vallejo's Water System," *[Vallejo] Times-Herald,* 24 May 1964, 16 July 1967, 12 Jan. 1969.

14. *The Resources of Vallejo* (Solano County Advertiser, 1869), 55; Gregory, 158; Leach, 157; *Vallejo Weekly Chronicle,* 3 July 1869, 11, 18 Dec. 1869; *Vallejo Evening Chronicle,* 3, 17, 21 Jan. 1870.

15. *The Prospects of Vallejo* (Vallejo: Chronicle Steam Press, 1871), 41; Leach, 158; *Solano Dir.,* 258; Gregory, 111; *Oakland Transcript,* 20 July 1872, p.3.; *History of Solano County* (Oakland: Wood & Co., 1879), 223-224; *Wkly Chron.,* 25 Dec. 1869, 17 Jan. 1870; *Eve. Chron.,* 3, 17, 21 Jan. 1870.

16. *Eve. Chron.,* 19 Feb. 1870; Wichels, 12 Jan. 1969.

17. *Eve. Chron.,* 22 July 1870.

18. Ban. Lib., Chabot File, "Letter, Lewis Shumacher [S.F.] to Paul K. Hubbs [Vallejo]," May 25, 1870.

19. Leach, 159; *Hist. Solano,* 223-224; Gregory 111-112; *Prospects,* 41.

20. *Eve. Chron.,* 5, 10 Dec. 1870.

21. C.A. Meneffee, *A Brief History of Napa...Counties* (Napa City: Reporter Pub. House, 1873), 110-111.

22. Leach, 159; *Eve., Chron.,* 15 Mar. 1870, 18 July 1874; Wichels, 12 Jan. 1969.

23. Leach, 159-160; Wichels, 12 Jan. 1969.

24. Wichels, 19 Dec. 1965; *Hist. Solano,* 223-224.

25. Gregory, 77, 80, 81, 84; *Vallejo Times Herald,* (Mare Island Centennial, ed.), 16 Sept. 1954. *Hist. Solano,* 223-224; Wichels, 30 May 1976.

26. Wichels, 12 Jan. 1969.

27. Gregory, 110-111; *Hist. Solano,* 224; Wichels, 16 Oct. 1966, 19 Jan. 1969, 13 July 1969, 30 May 1976.

Chapter 10

1. Burgess Thesis, 56-59, 69, 73.
2. Sherwood D. Burgess, "The Oakland Water War," *California History* 64:1, (Winter 1985): 35; *Oak. Dir.*, (1873-1884) s.v. Chabot, R.; Pierce Pap., "Marshall Pierce, Memoirs," Ltrs, "Marshall to son (Orestes)," Oct. 7, 1877 and Sept. 15, 1878.
3. Burgess Thesis, 35-37, 69, 102; Chab. Sch. 46; Burgess, "Water War," 35; Pierce Pap., Ltr. "Nan to brother (Orestes)," Oct. 10, 1877; *Oak. Daily News,* 8 Apr., 1874.
4. Burgess Thesis, 60-61, 94; M.H. Wood, *History of Alameda County* (Oakland: M.H. Wood, 1883), 652-653.
5. Burgess Thesis, 62-65.
6. Ibid. 66; "Caspar Hopkins Recollections," *CHSQ* 27:1 (1948): 71-72.
7. Burgess Thesis, 66, 98.
8. Ibid. 98-99.
9. Ibid. 93, 94, 99.
10. Ibid. 95-97.
11. Ibid. 100.
12. Ibid. 71-72, 85.
13. Ibid. 74-75.
14. Ibid. 75-76.
15. Ibid. 77-78.
16. Ibid. 79-80.
17. Ibid. 85.
18. Ibid. 102-108; Wood, 656-657.
19. Burgess Thesis, 109-112; Wood, 656-657.
20. Burgess Thesis, 112.
21. Ibid. 116; Wood,657.
22. Burgess Thesis, 116-117; John W. Noble, *Its name was M.U.D.* (Oakland: 1970), 46.

Chapter 11

1. *Oak. Dir.*, (Dec. 1874), s.v. Chabot, A., Tubbs Hotel, Tubbs, Hiram, Advt. Tubbs Hotel; *Times,* Obit.
2. Burgess Thesis, 85.
3. Ibid. 85.
4. Ibid. 112-113.
5. Ibid. 85-86, 90; *Times,* Christmas Edition, 1879, 4.

6. Burgess Thesis, 90.

7. Ibid. 88.

8. Ibid. 90.

9. Ibid. 86-87.

10. Ibid. 87-88.

11. Ibid. 90.

12. Ibid. 88-89.

13. Ibid. 89.

14. Ibid. 89.

15. Ibid. 114.

16. Ibid. 115.

17. Ibid. 116.

18. Ibid. 90-91.

19. Ibid. 80.

20. Ibid. 80-83.

21. Ibid. 83-85.

22. Ibid. 82.

23. Ibid. 69.

24. Ibid. 119-121.

Chapter 12

1. *Oak. Dir.*, (1878-79, 1884), s.v. Chabot, A., Chabot,Remi.

2. Pierce Pap., "Ltr., Marshall to son [Orestes]," Oct. 7, 1877, Sept. 15, 1878, "Ltr., Nan to brother,[Orestes]," Oct. 10, 1877.

3. Wood, *History,* 861-862; Mem. Rec., 379; *Times, Trib., Enq.,* Obits.

4. *Oak. Dir.* (1881-82), s.v. Chabot, A., Tubbs, Hiram.

5. Mem. Rec., 376; *Trib.,* 25 May 1952; *Trib. Illust. Ed.,* Jan. 1889; *Oak. Dir.,* (1881-82), s.v. Chabot, A; Chab. Sch., 41.

6. *Chron.,* 13 Nov. 1904; *Trib.,* 12 Nov. 1904.

7. *Enq.,* 5 Jan. 1888; *Times,* Obit.; *Trib.,* 4 Feb. 1888;phone conversation with Genevive di San Faustino, step-granddaughter of Ellen Chabot Bothin.

8. *Times,* Obit.

9. *Oak. Dir.,* (1884), (1886), s.v. Chabot, Remi; "Chabot Bible;" *Trib.,* Annual edition, Jan. 1890, p.6.

10. "Chabot Bible;" *Trib.,* 25 May 1952.

11. E.A. Davis, *Commercial Encyclopedia* (San Francisco: Ellis A. Davis, 1914), 386; "Chabot Bible;" *Oak. Dir.,* (1892 to 1916), s.v. Chabot, Mrs. R.; *Call,* 11 Sept. 1892; *S.F. Eve. Post,* 2 May 1896; *Chron.,* 26 June 1916; *Trib.,* 25 May 1952.

12. "Chabot Bible;" *Oak. Dir.*, (1877-78), s.v. Chabot, Robert; *Enq.*, 5 Jan. 1888.

13. *Trib., Times, Enq.*, Obits.; for full list of investments see Chabot's Will, *Trib.*, 4 Feb. 1888.

14. Mem. Rec. 375; Chab. Sch. 39-40. *Trib.*, Obit.

15. Mem. Rec. 375; Chab. Sch. 38-39; *Trib., Times, Enq.*, Obits.; "Checklist of Manuscripts, CHS Library," *Calif. Hist.*, 66:1 (Mar. 1987): 64-65.

16. Mem. Rec. 375-376; *Trib.*, 4 Feb. 1888, (Will); *Times*, Obit.

17. Mem. Rec. 376; *Trib.*, 4 Feb. 1888; *Chron.*, 14 Jan. 1888.

18. Mem. Rec. 375-376; Chab. Sch. 41-42; *Enq.*, Obit.; *Trib.*, 25 May, 1952.

19. Larry Weathers, "100 Years of Cranberry Farming in Pacific County [Wash.]," *The Sou'wester* [Pac. Cty. Hist. Soc.] 18:3 (Autumn 1983): 43; Lucille McDonald, "A New Gadget in the Cranberry Bogs," *Seattle Times*, 18 Dec. 1949.

20. Chab. Sch. 40-41; Weathers, 44; Pacific County [Wash.], "Deeds," F:413-429, Aug. 4, 1883, I:84-86, Sept. 1884 [from Larry Weathers' notes to author].

21. Frank Turner, "...Anthony Chabot Figure in Cranberry Story," *[Ilwaco] Tribune*, 18 Dec. 1952, and "Story of old Chabot Bog," 28 Aug. 1953.

22. "The Chabot Bog," *Chinook Observer* [Long Beach, Wash.], 29 June 1973, 4; Weathers, 44; Washington State University, "Extension Bulletin, 703," (Nov. 1978) 8-9.

23. Alameda County, "Articles of Incorporation, Pacific Cranberry Company," June 1, 1883; Mem. Rec. 375; Weathers, 44.

24. *Alameda County Directory*, (1876) s.v. Chabot, Robert; *Oak. Dir.*, (1877-78) s.v. Chabot, Robert; Weathers, 44-45; "Census Information, Pacific County, 1892" [from Weathers' notes to author]; "Chabot Bible;" Mem. Rec. 376; Ltr. "Elwell Chabot to author," March, 1988.

25. Weathers, 49-50.

Chapter 13

1. Mem. Rec. 378; Chab. Sch. 43; *Trib., Times, Enq.*, Obits.

2. *Times, Enq., Trib.*, Obits; 4 Feb. 1888.

3. Chab. Sch. 43; *Trib., Times, Enq.*, Obits.

4. *Enq.*, Obit.; *Call*, 11 Sept. 1892; *Chron.*, 26 June 1916; Davis, *Encyc.*, 386; Conners, "Pioneer Women of Alameda County," Scrap book, Oak. Lib. Hist. Room.

5. Mem. Rec. 378; Chab. Sch. 46-47; *Trib., Times, Enq.*, Obits.; Davis, *Encyc.*, 386.

6. Mem. Rec. 378; Chab. Sch. 47-48; *Enq.*, 5 Jan. 1888; *Trib., Times, Enq.*, Obits.

7. *Enq.*, 9 Jan. 1888 (funeral message).

8. *History of Chabot Astronomical Observatory* (1883?) one page, no author, Chabot Obs. archives; Chab. Sch. 44-45; *Enq.*, Obit.

9. *Hist. Chabot Obs.; Enq.*, Obit.

10. City of Oakland, "Ordinance #922," April 16, 1883; "Rules for the Observatory," Nov. 1883, (Obs. Archives Scrapbook.)

11. *Times*, 22 May, 1883; "Address by Mayor J. West Martin, May 21, 1883," (Obs. archives).

12. Charles Burckhalter, *The Chabot Observatory* (1916), unpg. typewritten monograph; *Trib., Enq.*, Obit.

13. "Chabot Observatory Admission Card," May 24, 1886, (Obs. Archives); Burckhalter; *Enq.*, Obit.

14. Burckhalter; Picture, Bancroft Lib.; *Chron.*, 23 Jan. 1888, 29 July, 1928.

15. Burckhalter; *Chron.*, 29 July, 1928; *Trib.*, 11 May, 1887, 21 Jan. 1888; *Enq.*, 1 Nov. 1892.

16. Burckhalter; Mem. Rec. 378-379; *Trib.*, 4 Feb. 1888 (Will); "Clipping, 1913" undated, (Obs. Archives Scrapbook.).

17. East Bay Astronomical Society, *Chabot Observatory and Science Center* (Undated information pamphlet).

Chapter 14

1. Mem. Rec. 378; *Times, Enq.*, Obits.

2. Mem. Rec. 376.

3. *Trib., Times*, Obits.

4. City of Oakland, "Certificate of Death, Anthony Chabot," Jan. 6, 1888; *Enq.*, 5 Jan. 1888; *Trib., Times, Enq., Chron.*, Obit; Mem. Rec. 377.

5. Mem. Rec. 377; *Trib., Times, Enq.*, 9 Jan. 1888; *Chron.*, 10 Jan. 1888; *Call*, 20 Jan. 1888; Visit, Mountain View Cemetery, Oakland, Plot #9.

6. *Trib.*, 4 Feb. 1888 (Will, Probate papers missing from Alameda County Court House); *Trib.*, 18 Jan., 9 Aug., 1888; *Chron.*, 10, 14, 20 Jan. 1888, 26 July 1904 (settlement of estate).

7. Sherwood D. Burgess, "Oakland's Water War," *California History* LXIV:1 (Winter, 1985): 35-41; *Enq., Chron.*, 14 Jan. 1903; *Trib.*, 16 Jan. 1903.

8. Noble, *M.U.D.*, 10-11.

9. Health Department, City of Oakland, "Return of a Death," Mary A. Chabot, Nov. 12, 1904, dated Nov. 14; *Trib.*, 14 Nov. 1904; *Enq.*, 15 Nov. 1904; *[Lynn] Evening Item*, 23, 26, Nov. 1904, (Lynn, Mass. Pub. Lib.); Alameda County, "Probate, Mary A. Chabot," Nov. 17, 1904.

10. Visit, Chabot Plot; "Chabot Bible;" *Trib., Enq.*, 29 Mar. 1890; *Alta, Chron., Times*, 30 March, 1890; *Times*, 1 April, 1890; *Call*, 10 April, 1890.

11. "Chabot Bible;" *Trib.*, 25 May, 1952; Davis, *Encyclo.* 368.

12. "Chabot Bible;" Visit, Chabot Plot; *Chron.*, 26 June, 1916.

13. *Trib.*, 4 Feb. 1888, 12 Nov. 1904; *Chron.*, 13 Nov. 1904.

14. Ltr. "To Author from Ruth Chaplin," [former librarian, Steep Falls, ME) Oct. 20, 1987; Bookplate, CHS Lib. "Brewer Collection;" Phone conversations, Author with Genevive di San Faustino of San Francisco, Step-Granddaughter of Ellen Chabot Bothin— Recollections of Ellen, Dec. 1986.

15. Alameda County, "Marriage License," Bothin-Chabot, June 3, 1909; *Enq.*, 5 June, 1909; *Chron.*, 5 June, 6 June, 1909; *Oak. Dir.*, (1904-1909), s.v. Chabot, Ellen; *Oak. Dir.*, (1908-1909), s.v. Bothin, Henry E.

16. Clippings from unidentified Santa Barbara newspaper, 11 Feb. 1965, and from *Montecito Magazine*, Spring 1984, (courtesy Santa Barbara Public Library); di San Faustino Recollections; Santa Barbara County, "Certificate of Death," Ellen Chabot Bothin, Feb. 10, 1965; *Chron.*, 12 Feb. 1965.

Index

Acequia, 98, 100
Agricultural activities, 145–152
   Cranberry bog, 148–152
   East Oakland gardens, 147–148
   Livermore Valley Ranch, 147
   Oriental gardens, Temescal, 147–148
   Tea culture, 147–148
Aquatic Park, 54
Artesian wells, 47, 99, 100

Battle, Brice, 6
Belize, 16
Benicia, 21
Bensley Company, 52, 56–57, 58, 59–60
Bensley, John, 43, 57, 58, 59
Biddeford, Maine, 60
Bidleman, Enoch, 77–78, 79–80
Big Four, 118
Black Point, 54, 56
Bloomfield, 41
Blue Rock Springs Creek, Vallejo, 106–107, 111
Boardman, William, 1, 87–89, 90, 94, 118, 120, 125
Bonner, John, 100
Booming, 30
Bothin, Henry, 175
Brannan, Sam, 22
Brayton, Reverend I. H., 81
Brice, Battle, 7
Broadway, 73–74, 75, 80–81, 82, 84, 85, 92–93, 96
Brooklyn, 113
Buckeye Hill, 31
Buckeye Ravine, 25

Caldwell, A. B., 24
California (mail steamer), 17
California Cotton Mills, 145
California Paper Company, 146

California Steam Navigation
   Company, 43
California Water Company, 119–121, 120–121, 134–136
Canadiens, 2
Carquinez Straits, 20
Castro Valley, 131
Chabot, Anthony (Antoine)
   Agricultural investments, 148–152
   Death and funeral, 167–169
   Death of first wife, 70
   Early life in Quebec, 2–3
   Gold rush, journey to
      San Francisco, 17–19
   Home in East Oakland, 140
   Hydraulic mining development,
      30–32, 41
   Industrial investments, 145–146
   Last illness, 166–168
   Marriage, first wife, 69–70
   Marriage, second wife, 95–96
   Marysville real estate activities, 42–43
   Mississippi Valley, 6–10, 13–14
   Nevada City mining activities, 25–32
   New Bern, North Carolina, 5–7
   New York City, 3–5
   Oakland Gas Light Company, 72–75
   Oakland water activities. *See* California
      Water Company, Contra Costa Water
      Company, San Leandro Dam, San
      Leandro Reservoir, Sausal Dam,
      Sausal Reservoir, Temescal Dam,
      Temescal Reservoir
   Philanthropic activities. *See* Philan-
      thropies and Charities
   Proposed oil pipeline, 63–65
   Proposed tannery in Quebec, 12–13
   Proposed water works in Milwaukee,
      Wisconsin, 61–62
   Proposed water works
      in Portland, Maine, 63–66

San Francisco water activities. *See* San
  Francisco City Water Works
San Jose water activities. *See* San Jose
  Water Company
Steamboat, 10
Texas, 14
Vallejo water activities. *See* Vallejo
  City Water Company
Will, 166-167, 170-171
Chabot, Ellen (A. Chabot's daughter),
  70, 85, 95, 96, 158, 166, 167,
  170, 174-176
Chabot, Elwell, 152
Chabot, Emelie Padey, 86, 94–95, 143-
  144, 150, 167, 173-174
Chabot Hall, 164
Chabot, James, 152
Chabot, John, 58, 154
Chabot, Joseph, 2
Chabot, Mary Ann Bacheller, 86,
  95–96, 142-144, 166, 167, 172
Chabot, Modiste, 166
Chabot, Mrs. Ellen, 66, 70, 71, 85, 93,
  166
Chabot Observatory, 159–165
Chabot, Remi
  Childhood, 11, 12–13, 14
  Cranberry business, 150
  Death, 173
  Gold mining, 14, 27, 37, 40, 43
  Marriage, 86–87, 94–95, 96,
    143–144
  Oakland water activities, 71, 77, 86,
    87, 93, 113, 120, 125, 136,
    139, 142
  San Francisco water activities,
    53-54, 58–59, 59
Chabot, Robert, 145, 151, 154
Chabot, Toussaint, 15, 144
  At Deer Creek, 26
Chagres (town), 16
Chagres River, 16
Chambly, 2
Charities. *See* Philanthropies & charities

College of California, 73
Contra Costa County, 74
Contra Costa Water Company
  California Water Company
    purchased, 135–136
  Franchise terms, 78–80
  Incorporation, 77
  Municipalization threat, 121–123
  Pierce becomes president, 136
  San Leandro Dam completed, 133
  Sausal Water Company
    purchased, 116
  Temescal Dam completed, 85–91
Coyote holes, 28
Cradle, 23
Cranberry Bog, 148–152
Crocker Company, 119

Deer Creek, 20–22, 24–26
Dexter, Henry S., 48, 57, 59
Dimond Canyon, 115
Dingee, William, 171
Dry diggings, 28

East Bay Municipal Utility
  District, 123, 172,
East Bay Regional Park District, 91
East Oakland garden, 148
Eastland, Joseph, 72–73, 74, 74–75
Edgcumbe, Joseph Collins, 103,
  106–108, 109
Ensign, George H., 48–49, 57–58
Erie Canal, 4
Eureka Hotel, 87

Fabiola Hospital, 94, 144, 155, 173
Family charities, 154
Feather River, 22, 43
Feather River & Spanish Flat Ditching
  Company, 34
Flumes, 29–30, 34, 38, 51-58,
  89-90, 101, 127-130
Fort Point, 54
Frey, John, 109

Fruit Vale, 76, 115, 116, 132

Galveston (steamer), 15
Gibsonville, 39
Gilson, J. C., 159
Gold Run Creek, 24
Grass Valley, 28
Ground sluicing, 30

Haslehurst, William, 119
Hasty, Betsy, 65
Hasty, Ellen, *See* Chabot, Mrs. Ellen
Hopkins Caspar T., 115–116, 119
Hudson River, 4
Huff, S., 119
Hydraulic mining, 32, 41, 130

Interest rates, 35
Islias Creek, 58

Jesuit school, 2
Jordan, W. H., 159
Josephine (brig), 17–19
Judson, Egbert, 146
Judson Manufacturing Company, 146

Keyser, Charles A., 42
Kilburn, J. H., 34

La Porte, 33, 35
La Presentation, 2
Ladies' Relief Society, 155
Lake Chabot (San Leandro), 103, 131
Lake Chabot (Vallejo), 108
Lake Merritt, 113
Lake Temescal, 91, 113, 114, 115,
    116, 117
Landers, Bion A., 151
Lester, Eli, 33, 39, 40
Livermore Valley Ranch, 147
Lobos Creek, 50–51, 52, 56
Long Beach Peninsula, 148
Long toms, 29
Los Gatos Creek, 101

Low, F. F., 57
Lynn, Massachusetts, 60, 86, 95,
    166, 172

McKenzie, Donald, 97–98,
    99–101, 102–103
McLean, Rev. J. K., 161, 168
McManus, J. F., 40
Manhattan, 3
Mare Island, 104
Marsh, John, 22
Martinez, 21
Marysville, 22, 41-43, 47.
    See also Nye's Landing
Mason, Nathaniel H.A., 102
Matilla, Captain, 18
Matteson, Edward E., 32
Merrifield, Azro D., 48
Milwaukee, 61-62
Milwaukee River, 61
Mississippi River, 7, 9, 15
Mississippi Valley, 4, 7, 8, 13–14
Mount Diablo, 21
Mountain Lake Water Company, 48, 49
Mountain View Cemetery, 168, 169
Municipalization, 121

Napa, 108
Napa River, 18
Neuse River, 6, 12
Nevada City, 25–30, 33-35
New Bern, North Carolina, 6
New Orleans, Louisiana, 8–9, 14–15
New York City, 3
North Carolina, 5
Nye's Landing, 20, 22.
    See also Marysville

Oakland, 72–84, 91, 93–94, 96, 113–
    114, 116–118, 120–123, 123,
    124–127, 130, 131–133,
    137–138, 140–142, 144–145,
    146–148, 150, 153–154, 157,
    159–160, 164, 167–169

Oakland and Alameda Water
  Company, 77, 79
Oakland Gas Light Company, 72, 74
Occidental Hotel, 71
Oregon (mail steamer), 17
Oriental gardens, 147

Pacific Cranberry Company, 150–152
Padey, Emelie. *See* Chabot, Emelie Padey
Padey, Martin, 94
Panama, 15
Panic of 1837, 10
Parks Bar, 20, 22-23, 41
Parks, David, 22
Penn, Mr. & Mrs., 25, 28-29
Pennsylvania oil fields, 62
Philanthropies and Charities
  Chabot Observatory, 159–165
  Fabiola Hospital, 94, 155, 173
  Family, 154
  Ladies' Relief Society, 155–157
  Miscellaneous donations, 153–155
  Religious Charities, 154
  Veterans' Cottage,
    Yountsville, 154–155
  Womens' Sheltering and Protection
    Home, 157-158, 170
Pierce, Ann, 60
Pierce, Henry, 2, 60–61, 65, 66, 69,
  77, 87, 113, 120, 125, 136, 143,
  146, 149, 150, 168, 171
Pierce, Marshall, 60, 139
Pierce, Nan, 139
Pierce, William, 60
Pioneer Pulp Company, 146
Portland, Maine, 60–61, 63–66
Presidio of San Francisco, 51
Puget Sound Iron Company, 146

Quartz mining, 28
Quebec, 2

Rabbit Creek, 33
Rabbit Creek Diggings, 33

Rabbit Creek Hotel, 33
Rabbit Creek steam sawmill, 36–38
Railroad House, 47
Railroads, 8
Real estate investments, 146
Red church, 65, 69
Religious charities, 154
Richardson, William A., 46
Richelieu River, 2
Rigby, Adoniram J., 36
Rough and Ready, 23

Sacramento City, 20, 21
Sacramento River, 21
St. Hyacinthe, Quebec, 2, 11
St. Louis, Missouri, 9, 13, 14
St. Louis Steam Saw Mill, 36
San Francisco, 15, 17–18, 38–40,
  42–43, 43, 49–54, 56–60
San Francisco City Water
  Works, 52–60
  A. Chabot made President, 58
  Certificate of Incorporation, 52
  Chabot resigns, 59
  Flume from Lobos Creek, 51–55
  Franchises from Board of
    Supervisors, 52
  Internal dissension, 57
  Merger with Spring Valley, 59
  Punping station near Black Point, 54
  Reservoirs on Hyde Street Hill, 54
  Storm damages flume, 58
San Jose, 85, 103, 108
San Jose Water company, 100–103
San Leandro, 113, 120, 125, 134
San Leandro Canyon, 75, 118, 121–122
San Leandro Creek, 75, 113, 118,
  119, 126, 132, 134
San Leandro Dam, 76, 121, 125,
  133, 134
San Leandro Reservoir, 123, 134
"Saucelito Water and Steam Tug
  Company," 46
Sausal Creek, 76, 80, 115–116

Sausal Reservoir,   116, 132
Sausal Water Company,   115
Sausalito,   46
Sawmills,   34, 36
Sebago Lake,   64
Shackleford, Daniel,   6
Shattuck, Frank K.,   74, 78, 168
Sierra County,   33, 35–36, 40, 41–42
Slate Creek Valley,   33
Sluice boxes,   30
Smith, Archibald,   39
Spring Valley Water
   Company,   48–49, 57–59
Stamp, C. H.,   25
Standish, Maine,   60, 64, 65, 67–70
Steamboat,   10

Tannery
   At New Bern,   6–7
   Proposed in Quebec,   12–13
Tea culture,   147
Telegraph Road,   74, 76, 79–80, 81,
   82, 84, 93
Temescal Creek,   74, 76–77, 79–81,
   82–84, 86, 87, 100, 118
Temescal Dam,   80, 84-91, 103, 112
Temescal Reservoir,   See Lake Temescal
Temescal system,   93
Texas, Republic of,   14
Thompson, John,   39
Tillinghast, William H.,   57
Townsend, Captain A. A.,   23
Treaty of Guadalupe Hidalgo,   14
Tubbs, Hiram,   125, 127, 130, 132,
   134, 142, 150, 153, 154, 168, 169
Tubbs Hotel,   124, 127, 140, 142, 145

Vallejo,   85, 98, 103–106
Vallejo City Water Company,   106
Vallejo, Mariano,   104
Vallejo Water Company,   106
Veterans' Cottage,   155
Von Schmidt, Alexander W.,   50-52,
   52, 53, 57–58, 59

Wages,   37
Water ditches,   29
Water rates,   92
Williams, B. O.,   35
Women's Sheltering and Protection Home
   of Oakland,   157–158, 167

Yamaska River,   12
Yuba County,   38
Yuba River,   20, 41, 42
Yuba river,   22